Miniature Embroidery

A FOUNDATION COURSE

Margaret Major

Miniature Embroidery

A FOUNDATION COURSE

Margaret Major

GUILD OF MASTER CRAFTSMAN PUBLICATIONS

First published 2005 by
Guild of Master Craftsman Publications Ltd,
Castle Place, 166 High Street, Lewes,
East Sussex, BN7 1XN

Text and designs © Margaret Major 2005
© in the work GMC Publications 2005

Photographs by Anthony Bailey
Illustrations by Penny Brown,
except pages 49 and 60 by John Yates

ISBN 1 86108 416 1

Production Manager: Hilary MacCallum
Managing Editor: Gerrie Purcell
Project Editor: Dominique Page

Designed by JoPatterson.com
Set in Berling

Colour origination by Altaimage
Printed and bound by Sino Publishing House Ltd

A note about the measurements
Measurements are imperial, with approximate metric equivalents in brackets. Please note, however,
that metric conversions may have been rounded up or down to the nearest equivalent. Only one set
of measurements should be used, either imperial or metric, and the two must not be mixed.

A note about the charts
In the keys to the charts, colour blocks refer either to tent stitch, half-cross stitch, Florentine stitch or
cross stitch, while colour bars refer to Rhodes stitch, backstitch, running stitch or Gobelin stitch.
Please note also that thread colour codes refer to the threads used in the projects. The colours in the
charts and the keys that accompany the charts are for reference only.

Dedication

To my ever-supportive husband Peter, my parents-in-law Jack and Kath,
and my sister Janet, with thanks to them all for their encouragement. Also, to my
daughter Elizabeth – my tireless proofreader and critic.

CONTENTS

Introduction

Most people are enthralled by small things, and miniature embroidery certainly has a fascination all of its own. It is an immensely absorbing and enjoyable pastime, but I know that even embroiderers that are very accomplished at full-size embroidery are sometimes a little apprehensive about starting.

The comment I most often hear from a would-be miniature embroiderer is: 'The work looks so fine that I couldn't possibly do it!' My reply is always: 'But of course you can.' However, you do need to know the basics, and I hope that I have covered every aspect of the craft in this book so that you can easily refer to the relevant section if you need help.

So, even if you have not threaded a needle since you left school, do have a go. I suggest you start with a fairly simple design, with not too many colour changes and a fairly low count of fabric. To assist you, I have graded each project as follows:

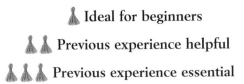

🪡 **Ideal for beginners**
🪡🪡 **Previous experience helpful**
🪡🪡🪡 **Previous experience essential**

All the projects in this book are 1/12 scale, i.e. one inch = one foot (25mm = 300mm). Work slowly and carefully and when you have finished, you should hopefully be pleased with the result. If not, keep it for future reference and try again. The cost of fabric and threads is minimal, so all you will have spent is a little time, and hopefully you will have gained confidence from the experience.

I do hope that this book will encourage you to embark on this very enjoyable and relaxing hobby.

Happy stitching!

GETTING STARTED

FABRICS

The basis for any embroidery is the fabric on which it is worked, and this is particularly important with miniature work, as some fabrics are more suitable than others. So, choose with care and you will almost certainly be proud of your efforts. In time, you will build up a small collection of different counts of fabric, so you will always have a suitable piece for your next project.

TIP Don't throw away scraps, as even tiny pieces of fabric can be used for your embroidery.

 ## *What does fabric count mean?*

This is the number of threads you can count across and down over an inch (25mm) of your chosen fabric or canvas, and will often be referred to as tpi (threads per inch) (25mm) or hpi (holes per inch) (25mm).

 ## *What types of fabric are used for miniature embroidery?*

Evenweave fabrics or canvas are used for counted-thread work.

 ## *What does evenweave mean?*

The term evenweave means that the warp and weft are woven evenly, so that the fabric or canvas has the same number of threads in both directions, i.e. 18 count will have 18 threads across an inch (25mm) and 18 threads down. Most people work from a coloured chart (or one with different symbols) when using evenweave fabric, and each square on the chart will represent one stitch over one thread of fabric, unless otherwise stated.

Evenweave fabrics

Which fabric should I choose?

There are many single-thread evenweave fabrics available in cotton, linen and mixtures of cotton with linen, rayon, polyester, etc.

LINEN

Linen is often easier to work on than cotton or a cotton mix, as the threads are finer, meaning the holes are slightly larger. This makes it easier to see where to put the stitches. Look out for Dublin, Belfast or Edinburgh linens, as these are ideal for miniature embroidery. Linens are often woven with threads of slightly varying thickness, and this can add interest to a finished piece that has not been completely covered by embroidery. (When working, just ignore the different thickness of the fabric threads.)

COTTON

Cotton is usually softer, and for items such as small cushions, chair seats and bed covers this is an advantage. Look out for cotton Lugana, Linda or Jubilee, all of which are suitable for miniature embroidery.

TIP Very small pieces of fabric are used for miniature embroidery, so it is always a good idea to buy the best you can afford. Synthetic fabrics, such as polyester or rayon, tend to provide disappointing results.

SILK GAUZE

Silk gauze is just what the name implies, and is generally used for small pieces of embroidery, such as cushions and chair seats. However, it can also work well for larger items, such as carpets, especially where a large amount of detail is required in the pattern. (The higher the count of fabric, the more stitches across and down and therefore the greater scope for design.) It is evenly woven and wonderful to work with, coming in counts from about 30tpi to very fine (over 100tpi), and is usually available in white and occasionally black. It is more expensive than other fabrics but can be bought in very small quantities, often by the square inch (25mm). The gauze has one great advantage over cotton or linen evenweave fabrics, namely that as the threads are very fine, the holes are larger and, of course, it is the holes you need to see! However, it is abrasive, so use short lengths of thread in your needle to prevent fraying, as the needle is pushed backwards and forwards through the gauze.

Silk gauze

COIN NET (CONGRESS CLOTH)

Coin net is a 24-count lightweight single-thread canvas that is ideal for wall hangings, rugs or carpets. It comes in different colours and has a very clear weave, making it easy to work.

CANVAS

Canvas is much stiffer than finer cottons and linens and is therefore very suitable for carpets and small rugs but obviously not for soft furnishings, such as cushions or bed covers. Most good-quality canvas is 100% cotton, and there are two main types available: double-thread canvas and mono-single-thread canvas. Single-thread, with a count of 18tpi or higher, is suitable for dolls' house embroidery. Lower counts need more strands of thread in your needle to cover the canvas, resulting in items that look too bulky and out of scale. Interlock mono canvas has threads that are bonded where they cross over each other, so it can be cut very close to the stitching without risk of fraying. Regular mono canvas has threads that are woven under and over each other, and it is helpful to bind the edges with masking tape before working to prevent fraying.

Canvas

BLOCK WEAVES

Block weaves, such as Aida, are frequently used for full-size embroidery, but I find them less suitable for dolls' house projects. Their threads are grouped into blocks that look like small squares with a hole at each corner.

Block weaves

 Are evenweave fabrics and canvases available in a range of colours?

Yes. The most commonly available are white and ecru, but many evenweave cottons, linens and mixtures come in a variety of other colours. Most canvases are white, ecru or 'antique' in colour.

Which fabric count works best for dolls' house embroidery?

Most embroiderers can see to work on an 18-count fabric – and many up to 40-count. A few are lucky enough to be able to work on much higher counts. As a general rule, 18–22 hpi canvas is suitable for rugs and carpets, 24hpi Congress cloth (coin net) is suitable for rugs, carpets, fire screens, pictures and wall hangings, etc. and 25–40hpi cotton, linen or silk gauze for practically everything.

TIP The greater number of threads to a square inch (25mm), the more detail you will be able to incorporate into a design, so it is worthwhile testing your ability on fine fabrics, as the results should be worth the effort.

Where can I buy these embroidery fabrics?

Many are available from haberdashery or dolls' house shops and others by specialist mail order outlets. Addresses for these can usually be found in magazines published for embroiderers, dolls' house enthusiasts, or on the Internet. Also see pages 152–154 of this book for a selection of addresses.

Are fabrics washable?

Some but not all. Some fabrics (especially canvas) have a stiffening agent in them, and water will dissolve it. Try to avoid the need for washing by keeping your unused fabrics and ongoing work covered when they are not needed.

Is it necessary to prepare the fabric edges before starting?

It is a good idea to protect the fabric edges from fraying. The simplest way to do this is to fold a length of masking tape over each edge. This makes a good firm edging into which drawing pins can be fixed if you are attaching your fabric to a wooden frame; it is easily removed when the work is complete.

THREADS

There are some wonderful embroidery threads available today – and in an amazing range of colours. When you see some that you like, buy a small quantity and experiment on various counts of fabric and canvas to see how they work. Building up a thread collection gives the same sort of pleasure as putting food in the freezer or logs in the log store!

 ## *Which threads work best for miniature embroidery?*

Many types are suitable, and the one that you use will depend on what you are making and on the fabric count. While silks and stranded cotton are probably most commonly used, it is also possible to use fine wool, which works especially well on carpets.

STRANDED COTTON
The best-known makes are DMC, Anchor and Madeira. They are each available in 8.7 yard (8m) skeins and are six-ply, meaning that each cut length can easily be separated into six single strands. So, by using different numbers of strands in your needle, threads can often be adapted to suit whichever fabric you choose. The skeins come in a wonderful array of colours and, although they are cotton, they have a soft sheen, so you sometimes hear them referred to as embroidery silks.

MATT COTTON THREAD (WITHOUT A SHEEN)
This is also widely available and may be more suitable for the particular item you are making.

PEARL COTTON
Pearl cotton is a softly twisted single-ply thread that is available in four main thicknesses: 3, 5, 8 and 12 (3 being the thickest and not really suitable for miniature embroidery). Number 5 can be used on 18-count canvas, 8 for 22–24-count fabric or canvas and 12 for finer work.

Stranded cotton and pearl cotton skeins

SILKS

Silks are usually more expensive than stranded cottons, but in miniature embroidery relatively small quantities are used. They have a beautiful sheen and are lovely to work with. Fine silks are available in single-strand skeins (i.e. not plied) and plied. They come in a wide range of colours and weights; choose the weight according to your fabric.

NB: The term plied is used when several strands of thread have been twisted together before being skeined.

Silk threads

 ## Can I use wool?

Yes, but I find it is best used when working on an 18tpi or 22tpi canvas. Medici is a fine wool that gives good results in miniature embroidery. Appletons crewel wool is a little more 'hairy' but, like Medici, there are some wonderful colours available. When using wool, always cut short lengths, no more than 7–9in (178–229mm), because wool frays as it is continually pulled through the fine canvas, and you will find there will be a difference in the look of your stitches if you use too long a length in your needle.

Wool

 ## Can I use synthetic threads?

Yes you can, and the colours of some synthetic threads are very tempting, but they are not the easiest threads to work with, as the tiny stitches are springy and don't usually lie quite so well. They also have a tendency to go a little fuzzy, so short lengths should be used. However, they do have a wonderful sheen, and it is always worth experimenting.

Can I use metallic threads?

Yes. Metallic threads are available in a large range of colours and come in several weights, the heaviest of which are designed to be couched into place. The finer metallic threads can be used in miniature work, but stitching with them is not easy, and it is probably better to keep their use to a minimum, i.e. for adding tiny detail. Fine metallic threads can also be added to your needle, with one or two strands of a fine cotton or silk (use short lengths to prevent it twisting and breaking). When using metallic thread for the first time, practise on a spare piece of fabric until you get a feel for how tight to pull the thread.

Metallic threads

What is random-dyed thread?

Also referred to as space dyed and multi-coloured, this is where skeins have been dyed randomly along their length, and these are readily available in cotton and silk. The skeins will usually have a general colour running through them with toning or contrasting colours added at random.

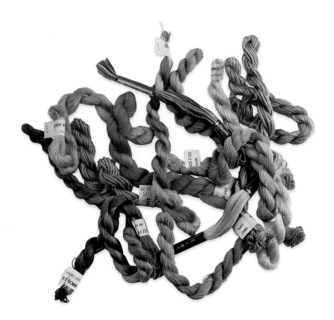

Random-dyed threads

They are very effective when used in miniature work, but as they will have been dyed for full-size embroidery, the variations along the length will probably be quite long. This means that quite a large area can be worked in miniature with very little colour variation. To avoid this, lay a fairly long piece of thread in front of you and cut a small piece where the colour variation is pleasing. Do this every time you need to rethread your needle. This can be a little wasteful (although, of course, you can save all the leftover pieces for another project), but it does ensure that the variations in colour are visible and will result in a unique piece of embroidery.

TIP When working cross stitch in random-dyed thread, finish each stitch before moving on to the next rather than working a row in one direction and then crossing stitches in the other direction. This ensures the stitches are formed from one colour rather than pink crossed with yellow, for example.

Where can I see a good selection of threads?

Specialist needlework shops, craft/needlework fairs and dolls' house fairs. Threads can also be bought through the Internet or mail order from needlework, dolls' house and craft magazines (see pages 152–154 for mail order addresses).

Are all threads washable?

Most but not all. To test for colourfastness, dampen some of the thread and press it between two sheets of absorbent paper. Leave to dry, and if no colour has transferred to the paper then the thread should be safe to wash at a low temperature.

What difference will it make whether I use cotton or silk thread?

The look will be slightly different, as silk usually has a higher lustre; otherwise, the choice is yours, as both will give a good result. However, do not mix the two in one project, unless you have designed something with that effect in mind.

What is meant by separating the strands and how can I do it?

Many threads are plied (see page 17), often resulting in a thread that is too thick for your chosen fabric, making it necessary to separate each strand. To do this, cut your required length of thread and hold with one hand near the top. Separate one strand from the others and pull straight up, ensuring the length of thread is not resting on your lap or on a table, enabling it to untwist as you pull. If you are using more than one strand, separate each one individually and lay them flat before threading them together through your needle.

How can I stop my thread becoming twisted as I work?

Hold your work upside down often and let the needle drop so that it can untwist. Alternatively, try using a double-ended needle. (See 'Needles', page 27.)

How long should my thread be and why can't it be longer?

For work on fine fabrics your thread should be about 7in (178mm) long and for canvas work about 9in (229mm) is appropriate. Using longer pieces of thread may result in fraying.

THE WASTE KNOT

When beginning a new colour, make a knot at the end of your thread and take the needle down from the front of your work a little way from (and in the direction of) where you intend to work. As you embroider, the 'tail' of thread will be covered by your stitches and after a few stitches the remaining tail can be cut and the knot pulled out.

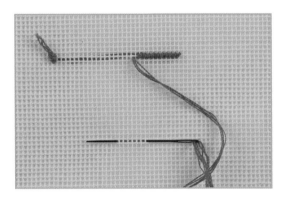

Waste Knot front

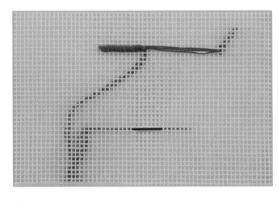

Waste Knot back

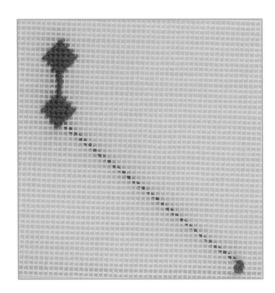

Away Knot

THE AWAY KNOT

If you are about to work an isolated motif, make a knot in your thread and take the needle down from the front of your work approximately 3in (76mm) from where you will make the first stitch. When the motif has been worked, cut the knot, rethread your needle with the 'tail' of the thread and work under the back of your stitches to secure.

LOOP START

This only works when you need an even number of strands of thread in your needle, i.e. two or four. Cut either one or two strands to double the length you want and then fold in half. Thread the loose ends through your needle at the same time, so that the one strand is now double in your needle and the two strands are now four. Bring the needle up from the back of your fabric at the position you want to start stitching. Do not pull the thread right through but leave a small loop at the back. As you take your needle back down, catch it in the loop and the thread will then be anchored. When rethreading your needle with a colour you have just used, anchor the new thread by taking it under the back of a few previously worked stitches.

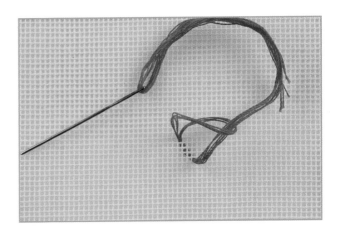

Loop Start

How many strands of thread do I need in my needle?

This will depend on what fabric you are using. Always work a small area on spare fabric, using the following as a guide for stitches that cross the threads of your fabric, i.e. tent stitch, cross stitch and half-cross stitch. The golden rule is to use just enough strands of thread in your needle to cover the fabric. Too few and the fabric will show through the design, too many and you will create unnecessary bulk. So, always experiment on a spare piece of fabric before you begin working your design.

Stranded cottons, silks or similar:	18tpi use 3 or 4 strands 22–32tpi use 2 strands 35tpi and over use 1 strand
Crewel wool:	18tpi use 2 strands 22–32tpi use 1 strand
Medici wool:	18, 22 use 2 or 3 strands 25–30tpi use 2 strands 35–40tpi use 1 strand Not suitable for finer fabrics

For straight stitches, i.e. Gobelin, backstitch and Florentine stitch, more strands may be needed to cover the fabric. When using a dark thread on a light fabric, it may be necessary to use one extra strand in your needle. If you wish to avoid doing this, consider painting the fabric with fabric paint before you start stitching. Choose a colour most suited for the purpose,

i.e. if you are working in mainly oranges, yellows and reds, a deep yellow fabric will show through the stitching less than the original white fabric, and if you are working predominantly with blues and mauves, paint the fabric blue. Use two coats of paint, allowing the first to dry before applying the second.

What is the best way to store my threads?

It helps to be fairly methodical with your thread storage. Use card or plastic spools for winding skeins onto, and always remember to write the make and colour number at the top. There are many plastic storage boxes available to fit these spools. It can be helpful to store silk in one box, stranded cottons in another, and so on.

The exception to this is the storage of random-dyed threads. To enable you to see the variations, leave these skeined and carefully pull out a length where the colour variation suits you then cut a piece to use. Done carefully, the thread should not tangle.

Thread storage such as this will keep your threads tidy and make it easy for you to find the colour you want

Can I mix threads from different manufacturers in one piece of embroidery?

Yes, but when mixing threads, make sure that they are of the same thickness (or use fewer or more strands in your needle to compensate) and make sure they have a similar lustre, unless you actually want a different look. Never be afraid to experiment.

How can I calculate the amount of thread required?

Usually, fairly small amounts of thread are used in miniature work, but if you have designed a large area to embroider in one colour, work a 1in (25mm) square on a spare piece of your chosen fabric, measuring how much you are using. From this, a rough calculation can be made as to the total required.

 TIP **Always buy sufficient thread before you start working, as colour dyes can vary. Ready-made purchased kits usually supply ample thread.**

FRAMES

Embroiderers tend to fall into two categories with regard to using frames while working: those who do and those who don't. Fortunately, with miniature embroidery, the frames are small and extremely light to hold; and while it is not absolutely essential, it is difficult to think of a justification for not using one.

Why do I need a frame?

When your fabric is properly mounted in a frame you will have a taut surface on which to build your stitches, the holes will be easier to see, the fabric will distort less, and your stitches will be more evenly tensioned. You will also feel more professional while working.

Which frames are best and will I need more than one?

There are many different types of frame on the market, so it is a good idea to have a look at some to see which will suit you best. Square or rectangular frames are better than round ones for evenweave work.

SOFTWOOD FRAMES

My favourite are the lengths of softwood, usually sold in packets of varying sizes and in pairs of the same size which slot together to form a square or rectangle. Decide on the inner measurement of the frame you need and, allowing at least ³⁄₄in (20mm) more on all sides than the finished project, simply slot the appropriate lengths of wood together.

These frames are inexpensive, lightweight, easy to pin your fabric to and can be reused many times

CARD MOUNTS

These are a good alternative for tiny projects, as they are light to hold, therefore reducing wrist strain. Use stiff card and cut a square or rectangle that is approximately 2in (50mm) larger than the embroidery to be worked. Cut out the centre, leaving a border of about 1–1½in (25–38mm).

LAP OR FLOOR-STANDING FRAMES

Larger lap or floor-standing frames can be used for miniature embroidery, and for these you will need to sew your small piece of embroidery fabric to a larger piece of waste fabric. When it is securely sewn, cut away the waste fabric behind the back of the embroidery fabric then attach it to your frame.

Building up a collection of card mounts, with different-size apertures, means you will always have a suitable one to work with

 Where can I buy frames?

From good haberdashery shops, craft fairs, dolls' house and miniatures fairs, the Internet, or look in miniaturists' and craft magazines for suppliers. Also see pages 152–154 of this book for mail order addresses.

 Are frames re-usable?

Yes, even the handmade card frames can be used repeatedly.

How do I attach the fabric to the frame?

When using a square or rectangular wooden frame, cut the fabric very slightly smaller than the frame and stick masking tape over the four edges to prevent fraying. Attach it with drawing pins through the masking tape at regular intervals, starting at the top centre then bottom centre, while pulling to make it taut. Work to the left of the top centre pin and then the left of the bottom centre pin. Then work to the right top and bottom, and finally the sides. If your fabric is not as tight as you would like, remove some of the pins and reposition.

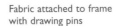

Fabric attached to frame
with drawing pins

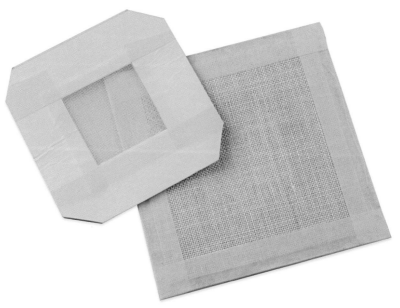

Fabric attached to card
mounts with masking tape

When using a card mount, the easiest way to attach the fabric is with lengths of masking tape that are quickly removed when the work is finished. Have the fabric slightly smaller than the mount.

NEEDLES

Using the right type and size of needle can make your stitching easier and improve the look of your work. Keep your needles safe (and away from children and pets) in a needle case, preferably grouped in sizes so that they are always readily to hand.

TIP It can save time to have two or three needles in use at one time – each threaded with a different colour.

Which needles should I use for counted-thread work?

Tapestry needles have elongated eyes, making them relatively easy to thread. They also have blunt ends, so there is less chance of splitting the fibres of the fabric or the threads of the stitches you have already worked. They are usually available in sizes 22–28 (the higher the number, the smaller the needle) and are suitable for canvas or fabrics with a count up to 35tpi.

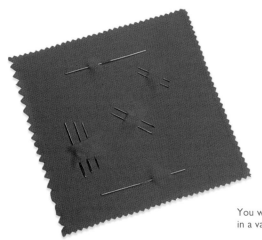

For 35–40 count fabric, I like to use a size 10 embroidery needle, and for 40–50 count, a size 10 quilting needle. A size 10 quilting needle is also useful for quick tiny stitching of hems on fine fabrics.

You will need several needles in a variety of sizes

How do I know whether my needle is the right size?

Your needle should hang in the fabric when inserted into a hole. If it falls through, it is too small, and if it needs a push to get it through, it is too large. The eye must not be wide enough to distort the fabric threads as you work.

Where can I buy needles for fine work?

Most haberdashery shops will have the range of sizes you need. They are also available by mail order (see needlework and embroidery magazines, plus addresses on pages 152–154) and the Internet.

What is a double-ended needle and do I need one?

No, but they can be useful. The eye is in the middle, with a point at either end. If you are using a hands-free frame, it is therefore possible to have one hand above and one below the embroidery and keep the needle straight the whole time. This means that you are passing the needle through the fabric without twisting the thread. However, they are longer than conventional needles and need practice to get used to. They are usually available in sizes 24 and 26, so they are not suitable for very fine work.

Are gold-plated needles better than nickel?

Many embroiderers prefer to use gold-plated needles, as they slip through the fabric easily, but they are not essential. They are less likely to leave a mark on your fabric if they are left in the work for any length of time, but they cost a little more. Platinum-plated needles are also now available at specialist needlecraft shops, mail order (see pages 152–154) and via the Internet.

I can't thread my needle. Can I buy something to help me?

Yes, there are many different types of inexpensive needle threaders available. Find one that suits you.

SCISSORS

Like carpenters, artists and bookbinders, embroiderers need their tools. Scissors are important, so buy the best that you can afford. With care, they will last you for many years – maybe even a lifetime – and can be handed down to the next generation.

 ## How many pairs of scissors do I need?

Two pairs are essential: a small embroidery pair with sharp points (that cut right up to the point) and a larger pair for cutting fabric. Keep your scissors sharp to avoid fraying the embroidery threads when cutting (making it harder to thread your needle) and to make a neat, straight cut in your fabric. Small scissors are easily lost while working so try tying a length of coloured ribbon to them. This also helps you to recognize your pair if you are working with other embroiderers.

You will need small scissors for cutting threads and large scissors for cutting fabric

What are snips and do I need them?

Snips are not essential but they are useful to have in your workbasket. The blades lie flat against your work and cut close to it. They mostly have plastic handles and blade covers and are inexpensive to buy. Most are similar in size and shape but do try them, if possible, before buying to make sure they are comfortable to use. They are very sharp so care should be taken when using them and, like scissors, they should be kept away from children.

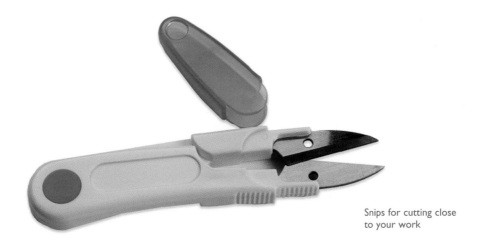

Snips for cutting close
to your work

What is a stitch ripper and do I need one?

Again, stitch rippers are not essential but they are useful for those times you need to unpick some stitches. A stitch ripper has a fine point that slips under a stitch at a time, cutting each one. (Take care not to slip the point through the fabric as well.) They are best used from the back of the work. A pair of tweezers can be useful for removing tiny pieces of cut thread.

A stitch ripper for unpicking stitches

MAGNIFIERS AND LIGHTING

Miniature embroidery is a wonderful hobby, enabling you to create many beautiful items for your dolls' house. The whole process should be a pleasure, but if you struggle to see where to place your needle for each stitch you may quickly become disillusioned. Fortunately, there are many magnifying aids available that make life a lot easier. Working in a good light (preferably daylight) also helps.

Do I really need a magnifying aid?

At some time or other most people do. You will enjoy your embroidery far more if you can easily see where to put your needle, and you are less likely to make mistakes.

What type do I need?

There is a huge variety available, so do take the time to find one that suits you. These will include floor-standing magnifiers and others that clip onto a tabletop or hang around your neck. Magnifying spectacles and lenses that clip onto your own glasses are easy to use. Some magnifiers have a light attached to them, and if you use a daylight bulb it is easier to see the true colour of your threads. Magnifying strips are also available to place over the chart you are following.

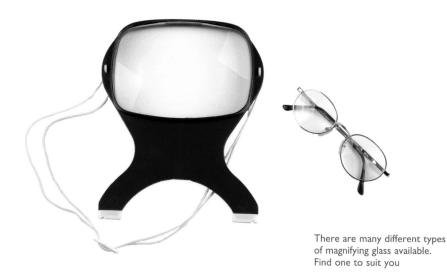

There are many different types of magnifying glass available. Find one to suit you

This magnifying glass
is ideal if you are
working at a table

 ## How do I know which is best for me?

Research what is available. If possible, take some fine work with you to see whether the magnification is adequate. It can be useful to have magnifying glasses that can be easily carried around with your work and a floor or table magnifier for when you are working at home.

 ## Where can I find them?

Haberdashery shops, specialist needlework and hobby shops, craft, dolls' house and needlework fairs, mail order from craft, needlecraft and dolls' house magazines or the Internet. (Also see pages 152–154.)

Do I need special lighting for miniature embroidery?

No, the same rules apply as with full-size work. When buying a light, choose the best you can and check whether it can be angled, raised, lowered, and so on. Some are free-standing, others clamp to a table. Some also have built-in magnifiers. If you intend to take the light with you on holiday or to friends' houses, for example, choose one that is not too bulky or heavy to move around, or one that can be partially dismantled for moving.

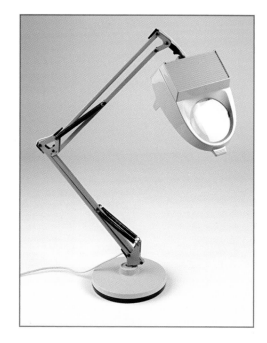

This light has a built-in magnifier

Is artificial light as good as sunlight?

In a perfect world we would all embroider in slightly shaded sunlight. However, since this is not always possible we have to resort to artificial light at times. Daylight bulbs provide a good white light and help distinguish between colours. They are widely available and although they are usually more expensive than ordinary bulbs, I think they are worth the extra cost.

Where can I see a variety of lights?

Good needlework and craft shops and needlework and hobby exhibitions. They are also available by mail order from advertisers in dolls' house, hobbies and craft magazines, or via the Internet. (Also see pages 152–154.)

HOW TO READ CHARTS

Charts for counted-thread embroidery can look a little daunting – but then so can knitting patterns if you don't know how to read them. You may find it easier to read a chart if you have it photocopied slightly larger. When reading a chart, remember that for tent stitch, cross stitch and half-cross stitch, the graph lines do not represent the threads of your fabric but are there to separate the colour blocks or symbols, and each coloured block or symbol represents one stitch. For straight stitches, such as backstitch, Florentine and Gobelin, the graph lines on the charts represent the fabric threads between which your stitches lie.

 Why do some charts look so much harder to follow than others?

Some charts are in black and white symbols instead of coloured blocks, and if the pattern is quite intricate the charts can look very confusing. Each symbol will represent a different colour, so they can be easier to follow if you go over the symbols in their respective colours. Some charts with black and white symbols also have coloured blocks.

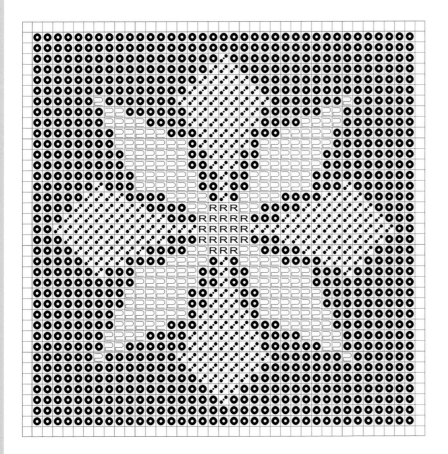

Black and white symbols chart

Probably the most popular charts are those that have a colour block representing each stitch, but even these can look very complex if there is a lot of detail in the pattern. Just concentrate on the small area you are working and count the stitches carefully to avoid mistakes.

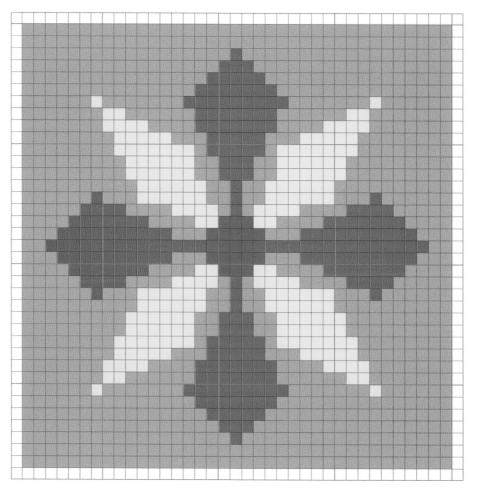

Colour blocks chart

 ### *Where should I start on the chart and does it matter?*

This is a matter of choice. Some embroiders like to start in the centre and work outwards, others work from side to side. For patterns with small motifs, it is often easier to work these first and then the background. When working from side to side, work from left to right if you are right handed and right to left if you are left handed, as this reduces the amount of time your hand brushes over your work, thereby keeping it cleaner.

Can I sell my work when I have copied a published chart?

Most published work is copyrighted. This means that designs cannot be used commercially without the permission of the designer and/or copyright owner. If in doubt, check with the publisher or designer.

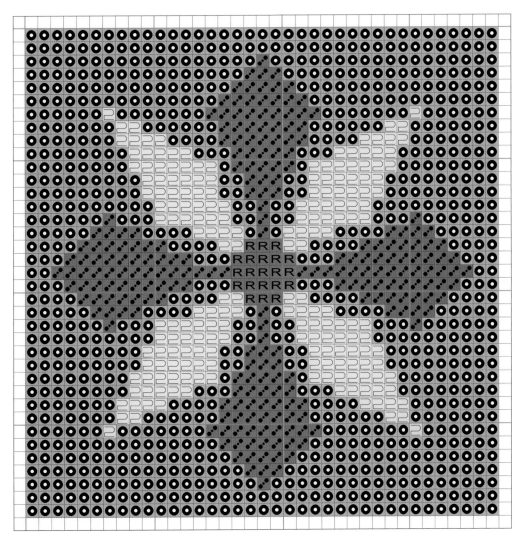

Colour blocks with symbols chart

KEEPING WORK CLEAN

A little piece of embroidery fabric worked on for hours with hot hands can quickly lose its new look! To avoid a crumpled, soiled appearance to your finished piece, always work in a clean space, with clean hands and relax. Work slowly and carefully, holding the fabric in a small frame to prevent it from becoming creased.

 Why is it important to keep my embroidery clean as I work?

Because of the finishes put into many embroidery fabrics and canvases, it is better to avoid the need to wash your finished piece. Also, while most embroidery threads are colourfast, they are not all, and washing risks ruining your work.

 How else can I keep my embroidery clean?

- *Keep your work away from inquisitive children and pets.*

- *Keep it covered when not working.*

- *Don't allow yourself to get too hot when working. Your needle and threads will become sticky, making it harder to work, and oils from your skin will stain light colours.*

- *Do not apply hand cream just as you are about to start work.*

- *Always try to use a frame, so that you are not actually holding the fabric.*

ACHIEVING A NEAT BACK

A good embroiderer takes as much care with the back of a piece of work as with the front. Try to always have thought for how the back is looking, and work your stitches with this in mind. You will be rewarded with a finished piece of embroidery to be proud of.

Why is it so important to keep the back of my work tidy?

For a start, everyone who handles your work will almost certainly turn it over to see how neat the back looks. Also, the front will look smoother, it is unlikely that odd tails of thread will work through to the front, knots which should not have been left will therefore not work loose, your stitches will be more even, and if you have to undo a few stitches while work is in progress, they are less likely to have become tangled in previously worked areas. I could go on…

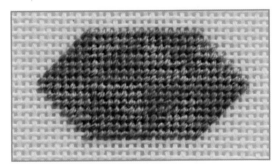

Embroidery from the front

How can I do so?

If the design you are working has several small motifs, work these first and the background last. Background threads can be taken across the motifs to a maximum of four or five stitches, or carefully woven underneath them.

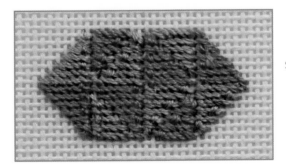

Same embroidery from the back

When a stitch requires several actions, such as Rhodes stitch, ensure you make each in exactly the same way. This will give continuity to the back and front of your work.

Start and finish each piece of thread with care (see 'Threads', pages 20–21). Trim each thread close to the fabric when it has been securely fastened. Do not leave little 'ends' which are liable to catch in your needle as you work future stitches, risking you taking a wrong colour thread through to the front of your work.

Can I trail threads from one area to another?

This is always best avoided, especially with dark-coloured threads, because these may show through from the front of your work, although there is less risk of this if the fabric is to be completely covered with stitches. If you feel you need to trail the thread, ensure that it isn't pulled too tightly, so that the fabric is not distorted.

Can I line the back of my work and how do I do this?

Yes, you may want to for items that are not going to be framed, such as dolls' house carpets, rugs and wall hangings, where the back is visible. Choose a finely woven natural fabric, such as cotton lawn or silk, in a matching or contrasting colour. Press the backing fabric to remove any creases and cut a piece the same size as your finished item. Press under a ¼in (6mm) border all around and place it centrally over the back of your work (wrong sides together). Secure with a few lace pins if necessary. With matching thread, carefully hem the two together.

Lining the back of
a miniature carpet

BLOCKING

Counted-thread embroidery often distorts during working and needs to be gently coaxed back into shape before trimming the excess fabric. If it is badly distorted it will need blocking to help it to regain its original shape.

Do I always need to block my work?

No. Some stitches cause less distortion than others, and some cause almost none. Also, there will probably be no need to block a piece of fabric that you have not completely covered in embroidery, i.e. where just a central piece has been worked on a bed cover.

Fabric that has become distorted and needs blocking

What do I need?

A wooden board and drawing pins, a sheet of clean white paper, plastic-film wrap, a pencil and a little water.

How do I go about it?

There are several blocking methods. The following works well, but first test the threads for colourfastness by dampening a spare length of thread and squeezing it between two pieces of absorbent paper. If no colour transfers to the paper, proceed as follows. **Do not trim the embroidery fabric.**

1 *Draw a rectangle on your paper (the overall size of your fabric), ensuring the corners are square.*

2 *Lay this on the board and cover with plastic film.*

3 *Secure the corners with masking tape or drawing pins.*

4 *Either spray your embroidery very lightly with a fine mist of clean water or dampen slightly with a moist sponge and lay it face up on the board.*

Board prepared for blocking

 TIP   Do not make the work too wet, as this will dissolve any stiffener in the canvas or fabric.

5   *Begin to pin it to fit the drawn shape. Start at the centre top and work to one corner then across to the other top corner. Do the same along the bottom, pulling gently as necessary, then pin both sides.*

6   *Leave to dry flat, away from direct heat. When completely dry, remove the pins. The work should now be the correct shape.*

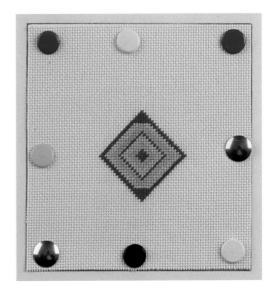

Fabric blocked

◆ What can I do if the embroidery threads are not colourfast?

Proceed as above without dampening the fabric. Leave for some days and repeat if necessary.

◆ Is it ever necessary to block a piece of fabric more than once?

Yes. If it is badly distorted you may need to repeat the above process again.

◆ Can I avoid the process of blocking?

A little gentle pulling to correct out-of-shape embroidery may work for tiny items such as dolls' house cushions. For miniature stools or chest tops you may be able to fix the embroidery on its base, correcting the shape as you go. But I would always suggest taking the time to block all items if they are out of shape.

MISTAKES

We all make them! Obviously, tiny stitches are not easy to undo, so they need tackling slowly and carefully and in a good light. Fortunately, it is possible to go over the odd stitch or two that has been worked in the wrong colour. Simply work the stitches again, over the originals, in the correct colour, pulling the thread fairly tightly so that the stitches don't sit proud of the others.

If you notice a recent mistake, you can usually undo the stitches one at a time by pulling the thread through from the back of your work. When you have done this, you will probably find that the thread has frayed slightly, so it is advisable to finish the thread off by working under nearby stitches and then starting again with a new piece of thread.

If the mistake is some way back, you will need to use a pair of sharp-pointed scissors or a stitch ripper to undo the stitches where necessary, but do take care not to cut the fabric. If the worst happens and you do cut the fabric – don't panic. Just apply a tiny amount

of fabric glue to the back of the fabric on and around the area you have cut. Allow this to dry thoroughly and you will find that, although the glue has filled the holes around the damaged area, your needle can easily be pushed through to form new holes, allowing you to rework the area.

Perhaps the best advice I can give to help you avoid too many mistakes, is to keep looking at the chart, if you are following one, count the fabric threads very carefully between motifs and try not to watch television at the same time!

QUICK TIPS

If fabric is creased, press carefully with a warm iron before embroidering.

When using stranded cottons or similar, separate the strands one at a time and let them untwist. Place as many strands together as you need then thread them all through the needle at the same time.

Count stitches carefully and, when using a chart, refer to it often.

For counted-thread embroidery, work each stitch with the stabbing method rather than taking your needle down and up in the same action. This keeps fabric in good shape and stitches even.

When working on very fine fabrics, hold your needle as upright as possible, as this will make it less likely for the needle to slip into the hole beside the one you actually want.

When your thread becomes twisted, hold the work upside down and let the needle drop and the thread untwist. Your stitches will be neater.

It is usually better to work patterned areas before background.

Use short lengths of thread to prevent fraying, especially when working on silk gauze.

- Use a needle threader if you find threading needles difficult.

- Work in a good light, preferably daylight, or with a lamp, fitted with a daylight bulb, beside you.

- Use only enough strands of thread in your needle to cover the fabric.

- Check out the many magnifying aids on the market and choose one that suits you.

- Try not to trail threads between one motif and another unless under existing stitches.

- Finish off threads by working under the back of several worked stitches, preferably of the same colour, and trim close to the fabric.

- Don't hold your needle too tightly: stitches are more likely to be pulled too tight if you are not relaxed. This will cause distortion of the fabric and the threads won't cover so well. Let the stitches lie smoothly on the fabric surface.

- In miniature embroidery, colours that are too similar blend into one another, making it difficult to see the pattern. When choosing your own colours, always ensure that there is enough difference between them. If unsure, work a small sample.

◆ *Keep your embroidery clean and covered when not being worked.*

◆ *Have regard for what the back of your work looks like – friends will always turn it over to look! Try to start and finish each colour under the stitches that are already worked in that colour.*

◆ *Whenever possible, bring your needle up through a hole that has not been used and down through a used hole. This will prevent threads being brought from the back to the front as you sew.*

◆ *When making up, work on a sheet of white paper. This will keep your work clean, and the corners of the paper can be used to check the 'squareness' of the embroidery.*

◆ *To help bed covers drape naturally over the bed, place a sheet of folded kitchen paper over the cover and then some folded aluminium foil. Tuck the foil down and just under the bed. Leave for a few days and you will find the bed cover is 'set' to the shape you want.*

◆ *Lastly, never be afraid to experiment. The costs with miniature embroidery are minimal, so if you don't like what you have been working, put it aside for future reference and try again.*

STITCHES
and
PROJECTS

STITCHING ADVICE

Not all recognized embroidery and tapestry stitches adapt well to miniature embroidery, but experiment for yourself. Remember, though, to use a stitch suitable for the fabric. A very fine fabric with a count of, say, 40hpi will not easily take cross stitch if you are working each stitch over one thread of the fabric. However, half-cross stitch or tent stitch will work well.

| TIP | Always try to keep the 'bulk' down. The effect should be as delicate and 'in scale' as possible. |

In this section, the working of the stitches is explained and charts show items embroidered under the various stitch types.

Which stitches are most useful?

Tent stitch, cross stitch and half-cross stitch are the most commonly used for counted-thread miniature embroidery, but Rhodes stitch, backstitch, running stitch and straight stitches, such as upright Gobelin and Florentine, also work well. All are best embroidered with a stabbing action (see 'Quick tips', pages 43). Designs can incorporate more than one type of stitch to good effect.

How tightly should I pull my thread?

Don't pull the thread too tightly, as this will distort the fabric and won't cover as well. Instead, let the stitches lie evenly on the surface.

TENT STITCH

This stitch covers the fabric well and provides a firm, neat back to your work; it is therefore ideal for carpets, wall hangings and chair seats. I use tent stitch more than half-cross stitch for my dolls' house embroideries, but the effect on the front of the work is very similar, so it is simply a matter of taste.

TIP Be aware that tent stitch uses more thread than half-cross stitch.

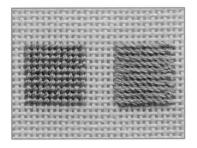

Sample shows how the front and back will look

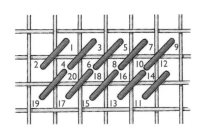

Stitches from left to right

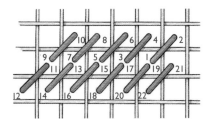

Stitches from right to left

Tent stitch can be worked, horizontally, vertically or diagonally, but I find that for small items, horizontal tent stitch is ideal. Bring your needle up at the odd numbers and down at the even numbers.

TIP If you are used to working in cross stitch or half-cross stitch, you may need to practise tent stitch a little before starting on your project. Use an easy-to-see 18tpi canvas and work a few rows to gain a feel for the stitch.

To complete each project see 'Making up', pages 148–151.

Seaside cushions 1 & 2

These two cushions can be used in a 1/12 or 1/24 scale dolls' house. Their bright colours and simple designs make them ideally suited to beginners. Work the motifs first and then the background, extending it, if you wish, to make a larger cushion. I have used three plaited six-strand lengths of thread to edge both cushions.

MATERIALS
◆ *Small quantity of DMC stranded cotton*
  350, 564, 602, 677, 722 and 798
◆ *27tpi evenweave fabric*
◆ *Tapestry needle size 26*
◆ *Backing fabric*
◆ *Soft stuffing*

DESIGN SIZE:
1in (25mm) square

STITCH COUNT:
27 x 27

STITCH SIZE:
Each stitch over one thread
of fabric

NUMBER OF STRANDS:
2

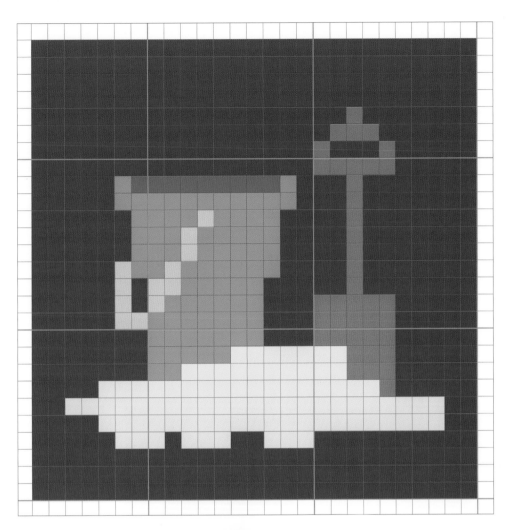

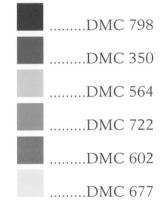

VARIATIONS

Try embroidering a wall panel for a nursery, using these two motifs and others of your own design – a bright yellow sun, perhaps, and a boat with a sail. A simple border would hold the designs together. (See 'Creating your own designs', pages 130–145, and 'Making up', pages 150–151, to finish the wall panel.)

COLOUR KEY:
Seaside cushion 1

.........DMC 798

.........DMC 350

.........DMC 564

.........DMC 722

.........DMC 602

.........DMC 677

MATERIALS

◆ *Small quantity of DMC stranded cotton*
  445, 553, 564, 602, 722 and 798
◆ *27tpi evenweave fabric*
◆ *Tapestry needle size 26*
◆ *Backing fabric*
◆ *Soft stuffing*

DESIGN SIZE:
1in (25mm) square

STITCH COUNT:
27 x 27

STITCH SIZE:
Each stitch over one thread
of fabric

NUMBER OF STRANDS:
2

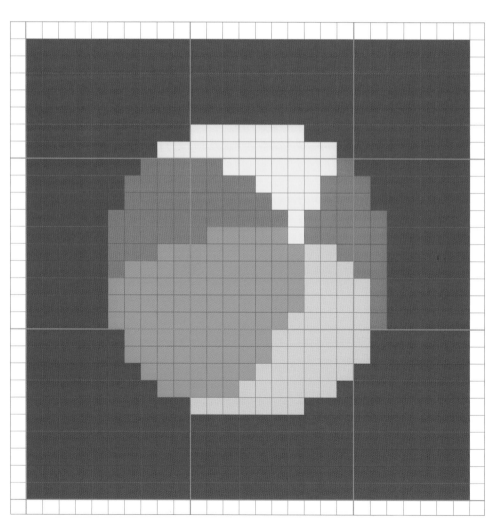

COLOUR KEY:
Seaside cushion 2

.........DMC 602

.........DMC 564

.........DMC 722

.........DMC 553

.........DMC 445

.........DMC 798

Pink & green rug

This geometrically patterned rug is fairly quick to work and the pattern can be reduced or extended to create exactly the size of rug you need for your dolls' house. Work the green area first then the pink background. I have folded the edges over and stuck them with fabric glue. For the pink edging, see 'Making up', page 149.

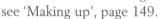

MATERIALS

◆ *2 skeins of DMC stranded cotton 3814 and 961*

◆ *18tpi canvas*

◆ *Tapestry needle size 22 or 24*

◆ *Fabric glue*

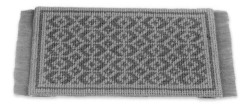

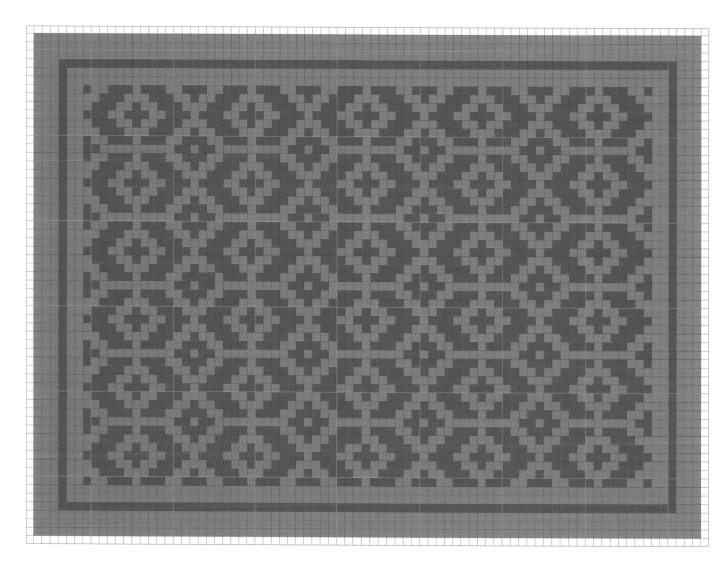

DESIGN SIZE:
Approx. 4½ x 3¾in
(115 x 95mm)

STITCH COUNT:
81 x 59

STITCH SIZE:
Each stitch over one thread
of canvas

NUMBER OF STRANDS:
3

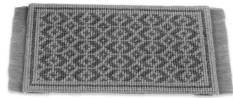

COLOUR KEY:

Pink & green rug

 ....DMC 961

.........DMC 3814

VARIATIONS

Try working this design in pretty pastel shades in the centre of a bed cover. Use 27tpi cotton fabric, with two strands of stranded cotton in your needle, and embroider the design in the centre, allowing extra fabric to hang down over both sides of the bed.

Mosaic cushion

This is a pleasing but relatively simple design to work, and is easiest to follow if you embroider the red shapes first, followed by the blue, and then the yellow. I have made a simple plaited edge, using three six-strand lengths of colour 3350. This cushion would look pretty embroidered in pastel shades for a bedroom.

MATERIALS

◆ *About ¹/₂ skein of DMC stranded cotton 3350, 3810 and 677*

◆ *25tpi evenweave fabric*

◆ *Tapestry needle size 24 or 26*

◆ *Backing fabric*

◆ *Soft stuffing*

DESIGN SIZE:
Approx. 1³/₄in (45mm) square

STITCH COUNT:
39 x 41

STITCH SIZE:
Each stitch over one thread
of fabric

NUMBER OF STRANDS:
2

COLOUR KEY:
Mosaic cushion

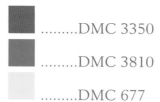

■ ....DMC 3350

■ ....DMC 3810

□ ....DMC 677

VARIATIONS

This geometric design is easily adapted to fit a stool or chest top; just continue the pattern until your work is the required size, allowing a little extra to cover your padding. A set of chair seats in this pattern would also look good, again working the pattern to fit your chairs.

Green carpet

Inspiration for this design came from a nineteenth-century dish from China, and I have kept the colours as close as possible to the original. The style of design is delicate, in spite of its intricacy, and the key border pattern (also on the dish) frames it well. I suggest working all the coloured motifs first, then the key pattern, and lastly the background.

You can take the background colour across small details of the pattern at the back of your work, but do not span more than about five stitches. Where there is a larger motif, take your background thread under it and continue.

MATERIALS

◆ *1 skein of DMC stranded cottons 677, 3350 and 3746*
◆ *2 skeins of DMC stranded cotton 3814*
◆ *5 to 6 skeins of DMC stranded cotton 3817*
◆ *22tpi evenweave canvas*
◆ *Tapestry needle size 24 or 26*

DESIGN SIZE:
7 x 5¾in (180 x 145mm)

STITCH COUNT:
159 x 135

STITCH SIZE:
Each stitch over one thread
of fabric

NUMBER OF STRANDS:
2

COLOUR KEY:

Green carpet

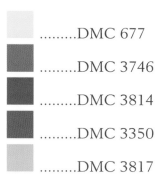

.........DMC 677

.........DMC 3746

.........DMC 3814

.........DMC 3350

.........DMC 3817

VARIATIONS

For a completely different look, try using alternative colours. I recommend you work a small sample of the pattern in your chosen colours before starting the carpet, so that you can see how they relate to each other. Spending a little time at this stage really does help you to achieve the look you are aiming for. (See 'Choosing colours', pages 141–145, for advice.)

If you would like a larger carpet, try working on 18tpi canvas, using one or two strands of fine wool or three or four strands of stranded cotton. The finished size will then be approximately 9 x 7½in (230 x 190mm).

HALF-CROSS STITCH

Although this stitch resembles tent stitch from the front, the back is quite different. The stitch is perfectly suited to miniature embroidery if you want a really slim piece of finished work, but it does not cover the fabric quite so effectively as tent stitch. However, it doesn't distort the fabric as much and uses less thread. Bring your needle up at the odd numbers and down at the even numbers.

TIP Do not pull the thread too tightly or the stitches will be inclined to slip between the fabric threads.

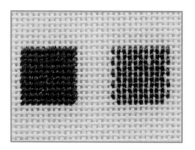

Close-up of half-cross stitch showing back and front

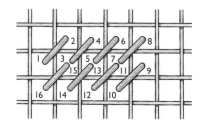

Stitches from left to right

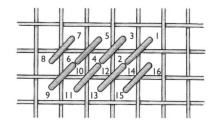

Stitches from right to left

To complete each project see 'Making up', pages 148–151.

Floral cushion

This stylized flower cushion is worked in soft colours and is suitable for a quiet sitting room or bedroom in your dolls' house. Work the pink and green stitches first, then the blue surround and, finally, the background, extending it slightly if you would like a larger cushion. I have used a very narrow ribbon to finish. If you would like a more dramatic effect, try using navy, a deep red and an emerald green.

MATERIALS

◆ *Small quantity of DMC stranded cottons 562, 813 and 3733*
◆ *About ¹/₂ skein of DMC stranded cotton 677*
◆ *27tpi evenweave fabric*
◆ *Tapestry needle size 26*
◆ *Backing fabric*
◆ *Soft stuffing*
◆ *Trimming*

DESIGN SIZE:
Approx. 1³/₈in (35mm) square

STITCH COUNT:
37 x 37

STITCH SIZE:
Each stitch over one thread of fabric

NUMBER OF STRANDS:
2

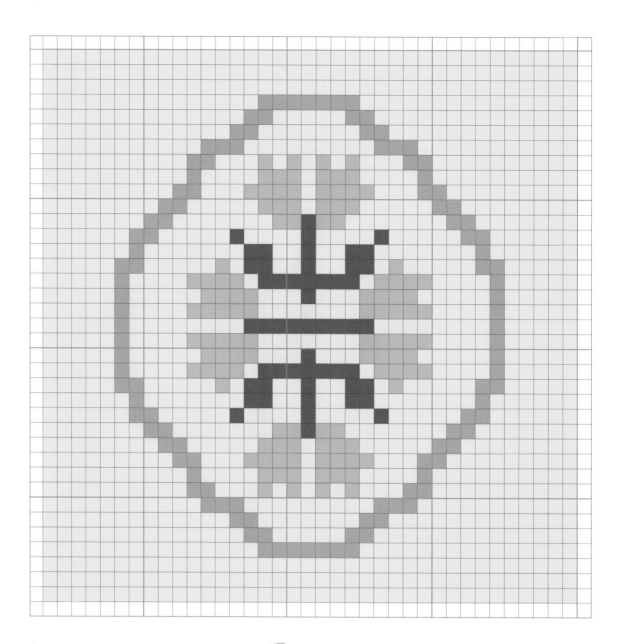

COLOUR KEY:
Floral cushion

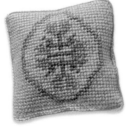

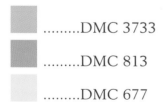 ....DMC 3733

.........DMC 813

.........DMC 677

.........DMC 562

VARIATIONS

This type of design has many uses, such as a set of embroidered chair seats, a stool top, or perhaps repeated two or three times to fit the top of a wooden chest. It can also be used to create a carpet design by embroidering the pattern at each corner, and perhaps in the centre too, using 24tpi coin net. By deciding how much space you want to allow between the motifs, you can make the carpet any size you want. (See 'Calculating size', pages 139–140.)

Bell-pull 1

This bell-pull, like the one on page 65, can be worked in an evening. It is useful for using up small quantities of stranded cotton. Finish with a tassel. (See 'Making up', page 150.)

MATERIALS

◆ *Small quantity of DMC stranded cotton 166 and 319*

◆ *35tpi linen*

◆ *Embroidery needle size 10*

◆ *Fabric glue*

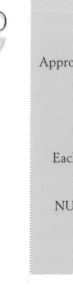

DESIGN SIZE:
Approx. 2¼ x ¼in (55 x 6mm)

STITCH COUNT:
75 x 9

STITCH SIZE:
Each stitch over one thread
of linen

NUMBER OF STRANDS:
1

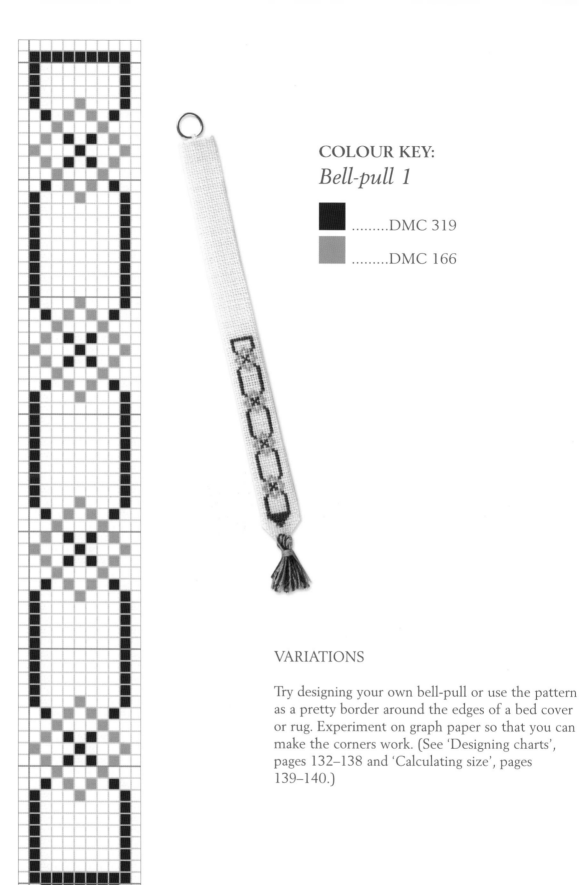

COLOUR KEY:
Bell-pull 1

■ ....DMC 319
■ ....DMC 166

VARIATIONS

Try designing your own bell-pull or use the pattern as a pretty border around the edges of a bed cover or rug. Experiment on graph paper so that you can make the corners work. (See 'Designing charts', pages 132–138 and 'Calculating size', pages 139–140.)

Bell-pull 2

Like the bell-pull on page 63, this one can also be worked in an evening. Items such as this are extremely useful for using up small leftover quantities of stranded cotton. Finish with a tassel. (See 'Making up', page 150.)

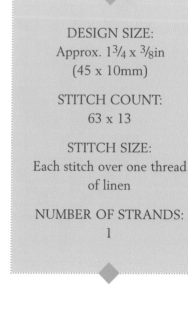

MATERIALS
◆ *Small quantity of DMC stranded cotton 553, 602 and 704*
◆ *35tpi linen*
◆ *Embroidery needle size 10*
◆ *Fabric glue*

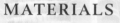

DESIGN SIZE:
Approx. 1³/₄ x ³/₈in
(45 x 10mm)

STITCH COUNT:
63 x 13

STITCH SIZE:
Each stitch over one thread
of linen

NUMBER OF STRANDS:
1

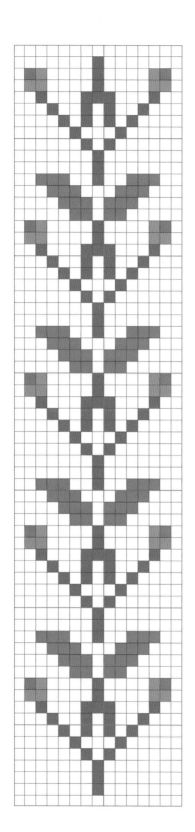

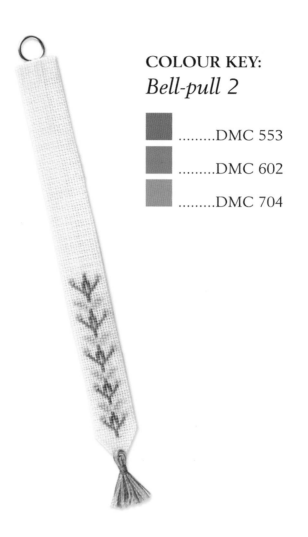

COLOUR KEY:
Bell-pull 2

█ ....DMC 553

█ ....DMC 602

█ ....DMC 704

VARIATIONS

This design can be used to edge plain curtains. Just extend the embroidery to fit the size of your curtain fabric.

Sunflower picture

This stylized sunflower is sure to amuse, and I really enjoyed embroidering it. Work the brown flower centre first to help with the placing of the petals, then the stem, buds and leaves, and lastly the urn. Finally, embroider the background to fit your frame in bright blue or a colour to match your dolls' house furnishings.

MATERIALS

◆ *Small quantity of DMC stranded cottons 223, 501, 725 and 3740*

◆ *About ¹/₂ skein of DMC stranded cotton 3752*

◆ *27tpi evenweave fabric*

◆ *Tapestry needle size 26*

◆ *Thin card*

◆ *Fabric glue*

◆ *Wooden frame*

◆ *Paint or stain*

DESIGN SIZE:
Approx. 2³/₈ x 1¹/₄in
(60 x 32mm)

STITCH COUNT:
63 x 35

STITCH SIZE:
Each stitch over one thread
of fabric

NUMBER OF STRANDS:
2

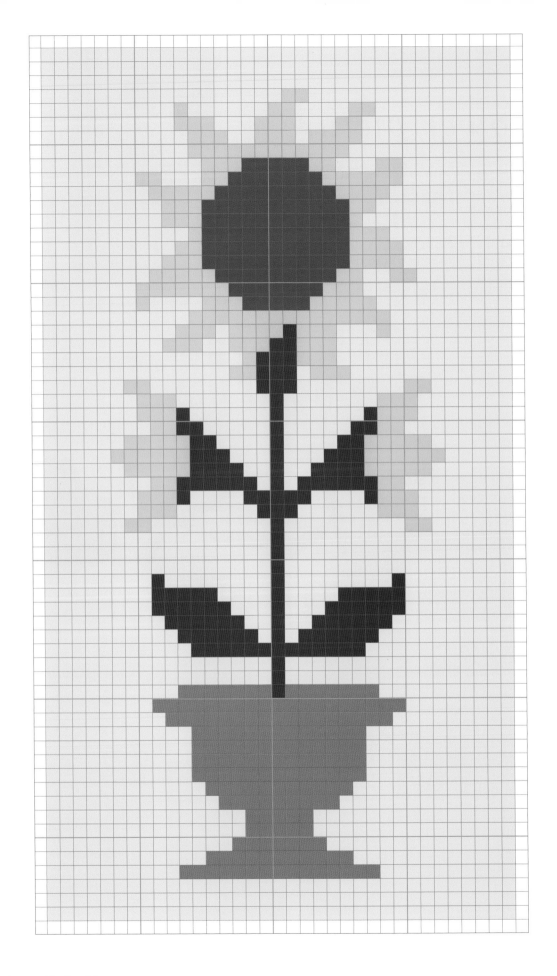

COLOUR KEY:
Sunflower picture

........DMC 223

........DMC 725

........DMC 501

........DMC 3740

........DMC 3752

VARIATIONS

I think this motif would make a lovely centrepiece for a single bed cover. Worked on 27tpi fabric, as above, the design size will work well, and a simple border, perhaps using colours 501 and 223, would finish it off nicely. (See 'Creating your own designs', pages 130–145.)

Abstract pattern fire screen

This design is loosely based on a picture of some agate jewellery, and with so many colours in the agate, I decided to use a random-dyed thread for the motif. (See 'Threads', page 18.) I have worked the background in a solid colour to give the motif more definition but, of course, this colour can be changed to suit your own colour scheme. Work sufficient background rows to fit your fire screen.

MATERIALS

- ◆ *Selection of fine random dyed silk threads*
- ◆ *1 skein of fine solid colour silk thread*
- ◆ *40tpi silk gauze*
- ◆ *Embroidery needle size 10*
- ◆ *Thin card*
- ◆ *Fabric glue*
- ◆ *Fire screen*
- ◆ *Paint or stain*

DESIGN SIZE:
2 x 1½in (50 x 38mm)

STITCH COUNT:
76 x 61

STITCH SIZE:
Each stitch over one thread
of gauze

NUMBER OF STRANDS:
1

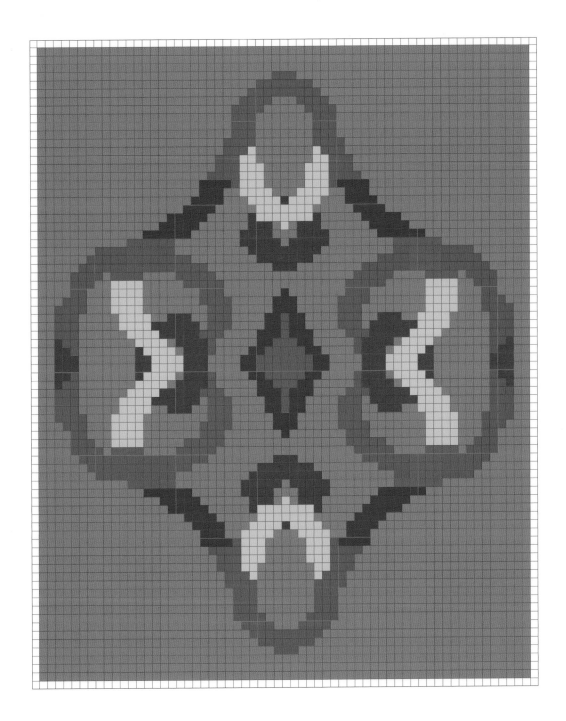

VARIATIONS

This abstract design would look quite different worked in solid colours rather than random-dyed threads. Try also using the design as a central pattern on a rug for a modern look. Worked on 18tpi canvas using two strands of wool or three or four strands of stranded cotton in your needle, the finished size would be approximately 4³⁄₈ x 3¹⁄₂in (110 x 90mm).

CROSS STITCH

This is one of the most popular embroidery stitches, with hundreds of cross-stitch kits available to buy. It is an easily worked stitch, but there are some points to remember.

1 *Ensure the top of each stitch lies in the same direction throughout, usually from bottom left to top right.*

2 *When working a large area of cross stitches, they can be worked in two 'journeys' i.e. all the bottom of the crosses in one direction and then all the top of the crosses on the way back. Bring your needle up at the odd numbers and down at the even numbers.*

3 *With very fine fabrics it is usually better to complete each cross before going on to the next.*

4 *You will find you can use less strands of thread in your needle than if you are working tent or half-cross stitch and still cover the fabric well.*

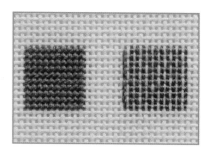

Close-up of cross stitch, worked to show how the front and back look

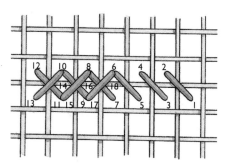

Cross stitch worked in two 'journeys'

To complete each project see 'Making up', pages 148–151.

Floral hall runner

I have used a very pale blue linen here, making it unnecessary to embroider the background. You can, of course, work a background colour around the design if you wish or use fabric paint on white linen in a colour of your choice.

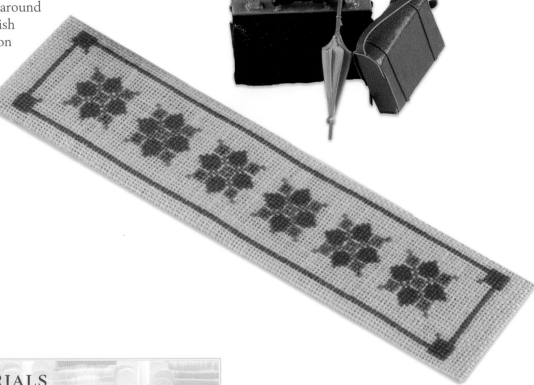

MATERIALS

◆ *Small quantity of DMC stranded cottons 718 and 3814*

◆ *28tpi Permin linen*

◆ *Tapestry needle size 26 or 28*

◆ *Fabric glue*

DESIGN SIZE:
Approx. 5 x 1⅛in
(125 x 30mm)

STITCH COUNT:
142 x 31

STITCH SIZE:
Each stitch over one thread
of linen

NUMBER OF STRANDS:
1

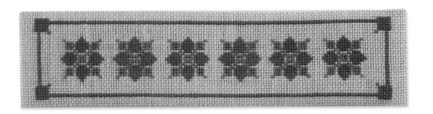

COLOUR KEY:
Floral hall runner

■ ....DMC 718

■ ....DMC 3814

VARIATIONS

One of these small motifs can easily be embroidered
on 25tpi cotton fabric to make a pretty cushion.
You will need to work five rows of background all
around to make a cushion that is approximately
1in (25mm) square. Just keep working more
background rows for a larger cushion. Alternatively,
try working several of the motifs to fit across the
top of a window seat or just one on each of a set
of dining room chairs, working sufficient rows of a
background colour to fit the window seat or chairs.

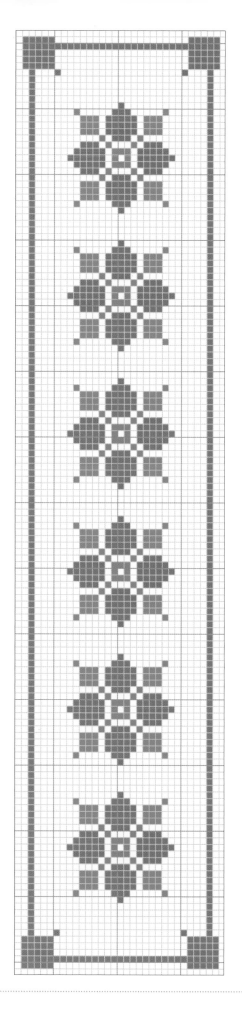

Floral fire screen

I enjoyed working this fire screen, for which I used a pale pink linen (Permin linen is available in many colours); this means that there is no need to embroider the background. However, you may want to use a white fabric and work the background in another colour. In this case, extend your stitching to fit your fire screen.

Work the large central flower first and then the green stems to help with the placing of the smaller flowers. Finally, work the urn and the fallen bloom.

MATERIALS

◆ *Small quantity of DMC stranded cotton 602, 680, 783, 3733 and 3818*

◆ *28tpi Permin linen*

◆ *Tapestry needle size 26 or 28*

◆ *Thin card*

◆ *Fabric glue*

◆ *Fire screen*

◆ *Paint or stain*

DESIGN SIZE:
Approx. 1⅝ x 1½in
(40 x 38mm)

STITCH COUNT:
41 x 39

STITCH SIZE:
Each stitch worked over
one thread of linen

NUMBER OF STRANDS:
1

COLOUR KEY:
Floral fire screen

- ....DMC 783
- ....DMC 680
- ....DMC 3733
- ....DMC 602
- ....DMC 3818

VARIATIONS

Use a 27tpi soft cotton fabric, such as Linda or Lugana, and embroider the motif to make a cushion. Choose colours to enhance the colour scheme of your dolls' house.

Flower panel wall hanging

The pattern for this delicate design is not difficult to follow, as it is broken down into small areas. Work the four flower panels first and then the green border patterns. I used thin imitation suede for the loops. (See 'Making up', pages 150–151.)

MATERIALS

- ◆ Small quantity of DMC stranded cotton 150, 402, 501, 503 and 3802
- ◆ 24tpi coin net
- ◆ Tapestry needle size 24
- ◆ Fabric glue
- ◆ Non-fraying material for loops

DESIGN SIZE:
Approx. 2⅝ x 1¾in
(65 x 45mm)

STITCH COUNT:
63 x 43

STITCH SIZE:
Each stitch worked over one thread of linen

NUMBER OF STRANDS:
1

Miniature Embroidery: A FOUNDATION COURSE

COLOUR KEY:
Flower panel wall hanging

■ ....DMC 501

■ ....DMC 3802

■ ....DMC 150

■ ....DMC 402

■ ....DMC 503

VARIATIONS

Each of the flower panels can be used to make a set of pictures. Choose matching frames that can be stained or painted to compliment the embroidery. Try also designing different pictures in the panel, perhaps stylized birds or trees, to make a wall hanging for another room in your dolls' house. (See 'Creating your own designs', pages 130–145.)

Pink framed sampler

Samplers are fun to work, but it is necessary to count the fabric threads carefully between motifs to ensure that they are correctly placed. Work the house first, then the flowers around it, and lastly the border. Change the colour of the house to suit your colour scheme. Remember to avoid trailing threads between one motif and another.

MATERIALS

- ◆ *Small quantity of DMC stranded cotton 316, 501, 503, 3802 and 3852*
- ◆ *27tpi evenweave fabric*
- ◆ *Tapestry needle size 26*
- ◆ *Thin card*
- ◆ *Fabric glue*
- ◆ *Picture frame*
- ◆ *Paint or stain*

DESIGN SIZE:
Approx. $2\frac{3}{8}$ x $1\frac{3}{4}$in
(60 x 45mm)

STITCH COUNT:
63 x 49

STITCH SIZE:
Each stitch over one thread of fabric

NUMBER OF STRANDS:
1

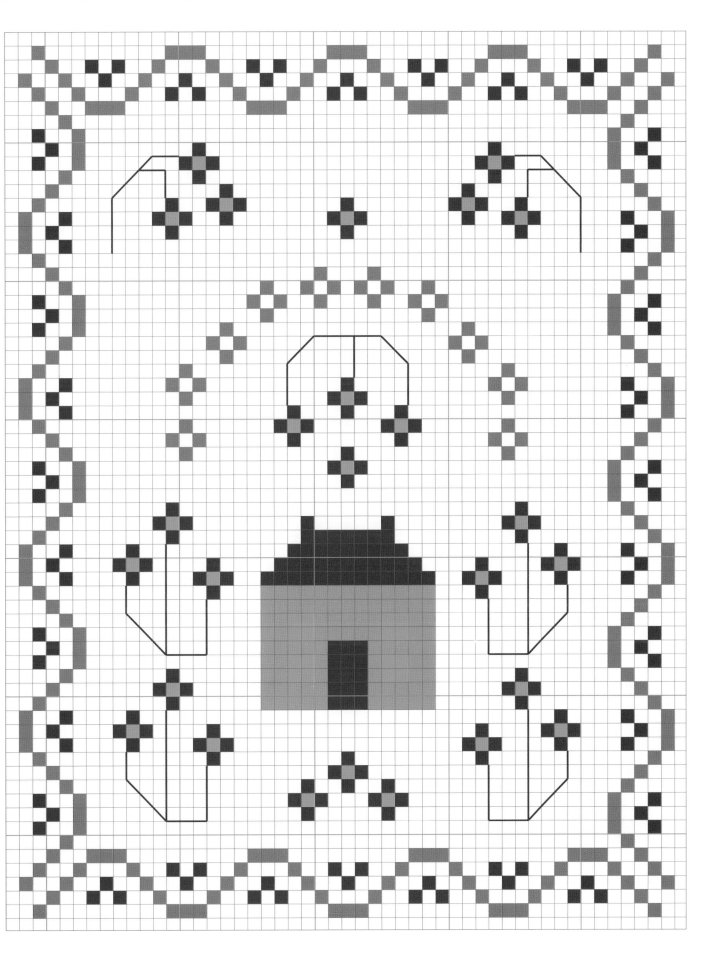

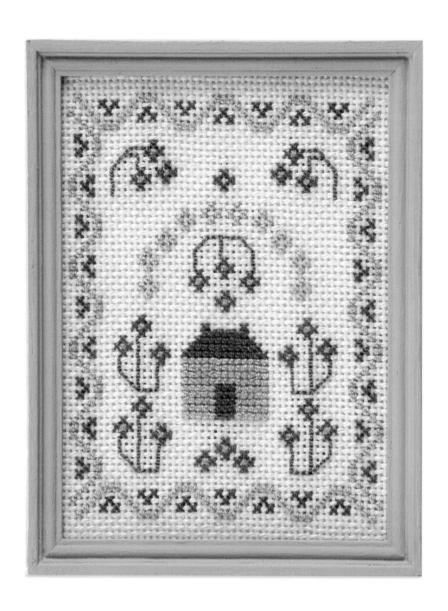

COLOUR KEY:
Pink framed sampler

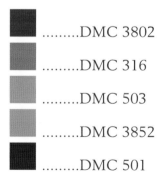

.........DMC 3802

.........DMC 316

.........DMC 503

.........DMC 3852

.........DMC 501

VARIATIONS

Try working a personalized sampler by including tiny lettering and a motif that resembles your own dolls' house. Add a border to hold the design together. (See 'Creating your own designs', pages 130–145.)

Sandcastle picture

I designed this picture as a reminder of many happy days spent on the beach as a child, when the sun was always shining.

TIP It is helpful to have several needles threaded at one time when working the sand, as there are lots of colour changes.

When the sand and castles are worked, embroider the sea and then the sky – not forgetting to put in that all-important sun.

MATERIALS

◆ *Small quantities of DMC stranded cotton 336, 350, 680, 726, 742, 798, 3820*

◆ *About $^1/_2$ skein of 3840*

◆ *27tpi evenweave fabric*

◆ *Tapestry needle size 26*

◆ *Thin card*

◆ *Fabric glue*

◆ *Wooden frame*

◆ *Paint or stain*

DESIGN SIZE:
Approx. $1^3/_4$ x $1^1/_4$in
(45 x 32mm)

STITCH COUNT:
48 x 34

STITCH SIZE:
Each stitch worked over one thread of fabric

NUMBER OF STRANDS:
1

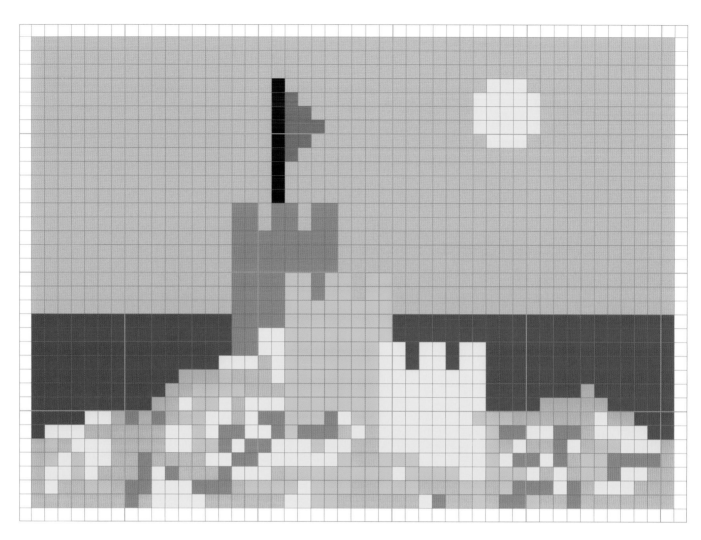

COLOUR KEY:
Sandcastle picture

………DMC 726

………DMC 3820

………DMC 742

………DMC 680

………DMC 350

………DMC 3840

………DMC 336

………DMC 798

VARIATIONS

This picture can be extended by taking the sand out further on both sides and perhaps adding a small boat to the water. Try designing the extra width on graph paper before embroidering. (See 'Creating your own designs', pages 130–145.)

RHODES STITCH

This lovely stitch gives a raised star effect that catches the light. In full-size embroidery, the stitch can be worked over a large number of threads, but for dolls' houses, embroidering the stitches over three threads works well.

Rhodes stitch is quick and easy to work. Simply bring the needle up at the odd numbers and down at the even ones; this ensures that there are long stitches at the back, which provide a padded effect. Practise on a piece of 18tpi canvas, working every stitch in the same sequence so that the top thread always lies in the same direction. Rhodes stitch can be used in conjunction with tent stitch, perhaps a series of three rows of three Rhodes stitches, with each group of nine interspersed with a row of tent stitch. (See *Miniature Embroidered Patchwork: Projects in 1/12 Scale*, Guild of Master Craftsman Publications, ISBN 1-86108-341-6.) Be warned: Rhodes stitch is addictive!

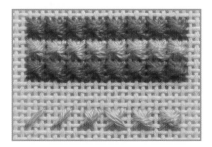

Close-up of Rhodes stitch

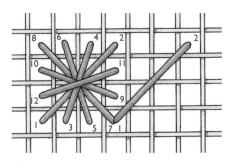

Rhodes stitch showing position of ajoining stitch

To complete each project see 'Making up', pages 148–151.

Cot cover

This cot cover is fairly easy to work, but do practise Rhodes stitch on a lower-count fabric if it is new to you. Each 'star' on the chart represents one Rhodes stitch over three threads of fabric. Once mastered, you will find it covers the fabric quickly.

Work all the inner Rhodes stitches, then the tent stitch all around, and lastly the outside row of Rhodes stitches. I backed the cover with a pale-coloured silk fabric.

MATERIALS

◆ *1 skein DMC stranded cotton 523 and 3771*
◆ *30tpi silk gauze*
◆ *Tapestry needle size 28*
◆ *Lightweight backing material*

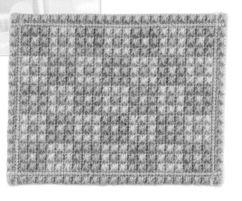

DESIGN SIZE:
Approx. 2¼ x 1¾in
(55 x 45mm)

STITCH COUNT:
71 x 53

STITCH SIZE:
Rhodes stitches over three threads of gauze and tent stitches over one thread of gauze

NUMBER OF STRANDS:
1 for Rhodes stitches and 2 for tent stitches

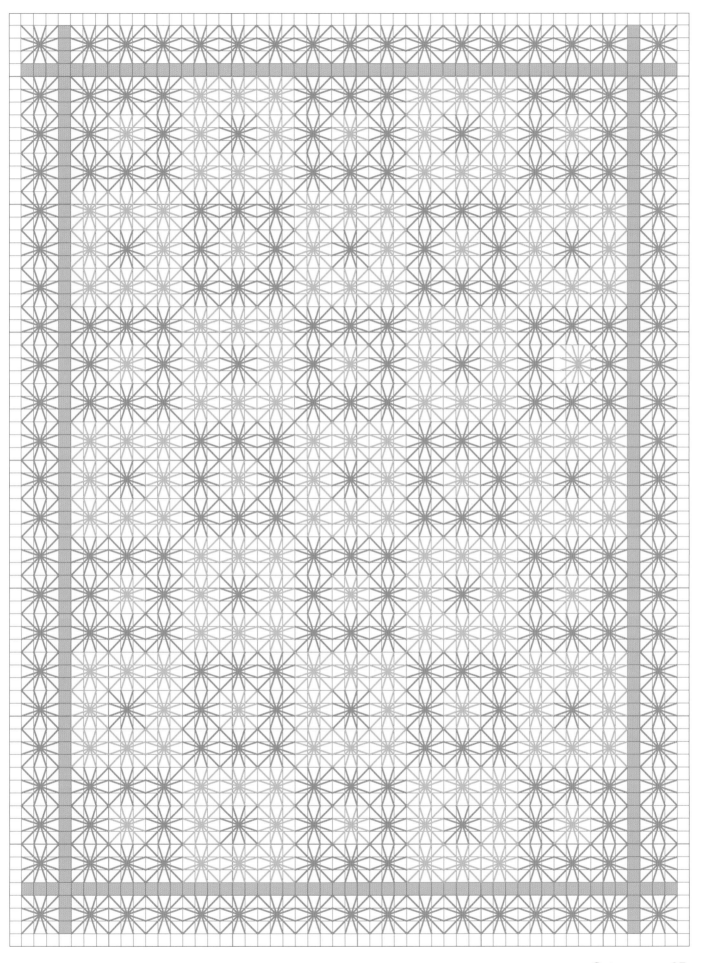

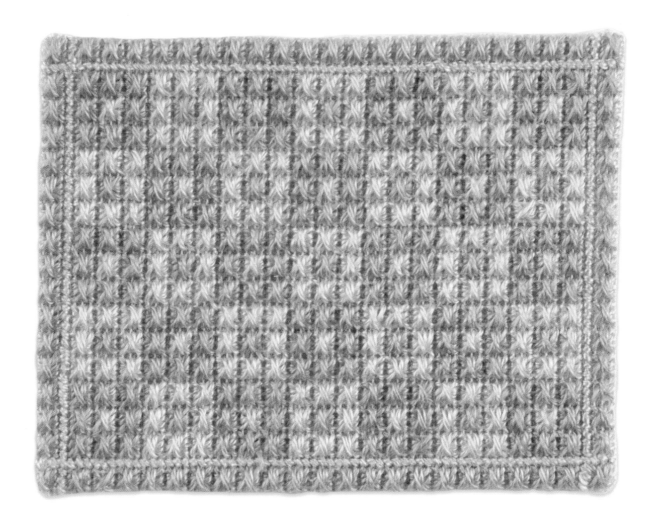

COLOUR KEY:

Cot cover

 ....DMC 3771

────────── ....DMC 523

────────── ....DMC 3771

VARIATIONS

Work five groups of nine Rhodes stitches across and down to make a cushion that is approximately 1¹⁄₂in (38mm) square , perhaps in different combinations of colours to make a set of cushions. By extending the number of rows of Rhodes stitches across and down, you can make a bed cover to sit on top of a single or double bed, maybe choosing colours to match an existing valance.

Padded chest top

The design on this chest top can be adapted to fit any chest by increasing or decreasing the number of background stitches, but do ensure that the motifs remain central. Work just a little more than the dimensions of the chest top to allow for the padding. I have attached two different braids around the edge, first a red ribbon and then a fine gold braid, but the choice is yours.

MATERIALS

- *2 skeins of DMC stranded cotton 309*
- *Small quantity of DMC stranded cotton 501 and 3820*
- *27tpi evenweave fabric*
- *Tapestry needle size 26*
- *Thin wadding or similar*
- *Thin card*
- *Fabric glue*
- *Wooden chest*
- *Paint or stain if necessary*

DESIGN SIZE:
Approx. 3³/₄ x 3in (95 x 76mm)

STITCH COUNT:
99 x 51

STITCH SIZE:
Each stitch over three threads of fabric

NUMBER OF STRANDS:
2

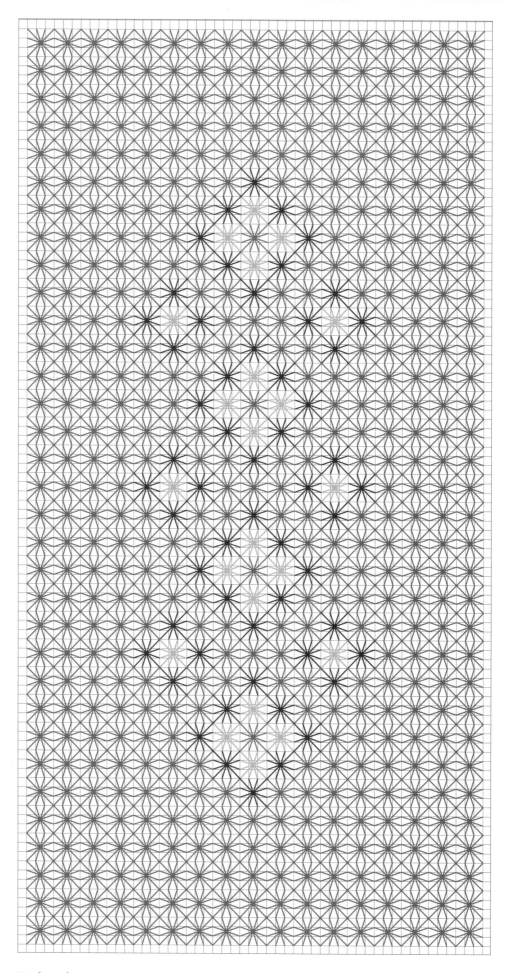

COLOUR KEY:
Padded chest top

▰▰▰ ....DMC 309

▰▰▰ ....DMC 501

▰▰▰ ....DMC 3820

VARIATIONS

Consider using this design to embroider a top for a window seat or use just the four central motifs for a cushion, working sufficient background colour until the seat top or cushion measures the size you want.

BACKSTITCH AND BLACKWORK

Backstitch is one of the simplest stitches to work, and the result can be a relatively simple one, as with the flower picture on page 94, or more intricate, as in the blackwork examples in this chapter, some of which also include cross stitch. Backstitch is also useful for outlining shapes worked in other stitches. For this you use the same holes as the previous stitches, so that the outline touches them.

TIP Don't pull the stitches too tightly as you work, as this will cause them to disappear between the fabric threads. Also, avoid trailing threads between motifs, as they could show through from the front.

Bring your needle up at the odd numbers and down at the even numbers. Where the stitch lines on the chart are more than one stitch long, work several stitches, each over one thread of fabric, rather than taking the thread straight across two or more fabric threads. This provides a neater look for miniature embroidery.

Blackwork is a fascinating technique and is traditionally worked on light-coloured fabrics, often white or ecru, so that the black stitches are shown to their best advantage. Backstitch creates many of the patterns, while cross stitch and other stitches can be included. The interest is created by varying the intensity of the stitch patterns, so that some appear lighter than others. There are many infill designs that work well in miniature (see 'Creating your own designs', pages 130–145). Try also using colour in 'blackwork' as with the Blackwork Wall Hanging on page 108.

TIP Remember, when reading a chart for straight stitches, such as backstitch, the graph lines on the chart represent the threads of the fabric and the stitches lie between them. (See 'How to read charts', pages 33–35.)

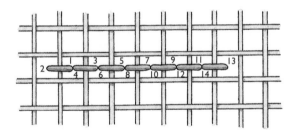

Close-up of backstitch

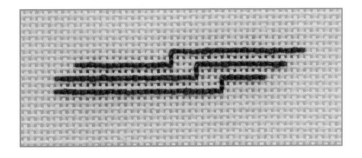

Backstitch, showing how each stitch lies between the fabric threads

To complete each project see 'Making up', pages 148–151.

Backstitch flower picture

This stylized flower picture is only an evening's work, and it makes a cheery addition to a dolls' house. I used a white fabric and painted it yellow with two coats of fabric paint, allowing it to dry between coats; this has the effect of stiffening the fabric slightly, making it easier to work. Don't worry about the holes filling with paint – they won't. When you have painted a fabric with your choice of colour, there is no need to embroider the background.

MATERIALS

◆ *Small quantity of DMC stranded cotton*
  700 and 817
◆ *32tpi evenweave fabric*
◆ *Tapestry needle size 28*
◆ *Thin card*
◆ *Fabric glue*
◆ *Wooden picture frame*
◆ *Paint or stain*

DESIGN SIZE:
1³/₄ x 1¹/₈in
(45 x 30mm) approx.

STITCH COUNT:
57 x 37

STITCH SIZE:
Each stitch over one thread
of fabric

NUMBER OF STRANDS:
1

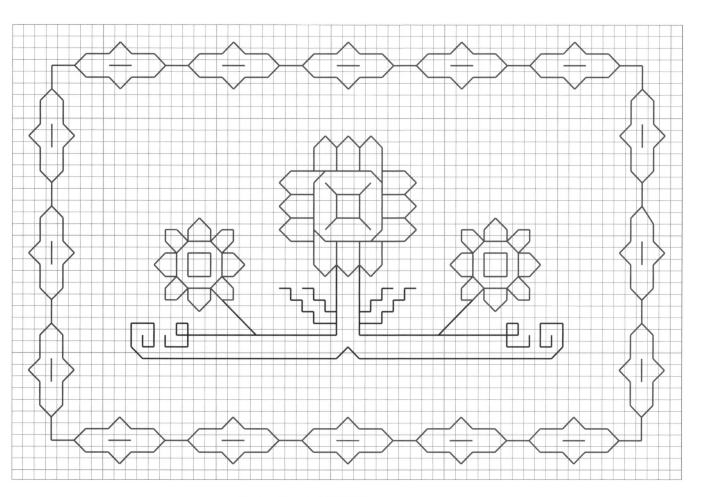

COLOUR KEY:
Backstitch flower picture

————— ....DMC 817

————— ....DMC 700

VARIATIONS

Try designing another small picture with a pretty border around it (see 'Creating your own designs, pages 130–145). A pair of stylized pictures both with painted, unworked backgrounds would look quite special in a modern house.

Blackwork cushions 1 & 2

I think these cushions demonstrate how a simple, repetitive blackwork pattern can look really effective. Try others for yourself. (See 'Creating your own designs', pages 130–145.) Both cushions are quick to work, as there is no background stitching. The finished size of the cushions depends on how much fabric you leave around the design. I embroidered both cushions on the same piece of fabric, leaving space in between for turnings on each.

For cushion 2, use 10in (255mm) lengths of thread and finish each motif by running your thread under the back of the stitches. (Do not trail the thread between motifs.) For cushion 1, use short lengths of thread and finish under the worked stitches. I have used three six-strand lengths of thread, plaited together, to edge the cushions.

MATERIALS

◆ *Small quantity of DMC stranded cotton 310*
◆ *27tpi evenweave fabric*
◆ *Tapestry needle size 26*
◆ *Thin backing material*
◆ *Soft stuffing*

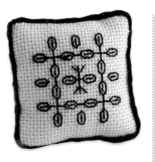

DESIGN SIZE:
Approx. 1in (25mm) square

STITCH COUNT:
cushion 1 = 27 x 27
cushion 2 = 28 x 28

STITCH SIZE:
Each stitch over one thread
of fabric

NUMBER OF STRANDS:
1

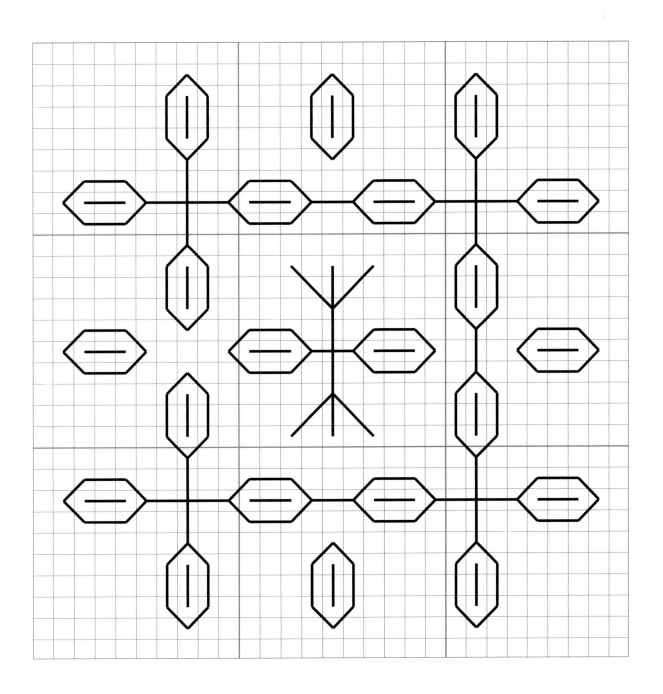

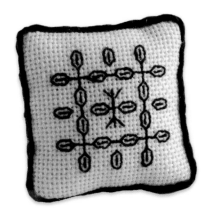

COLOUR KEY:

Blackwork cushion 1

━━━━━ ....DMC 310

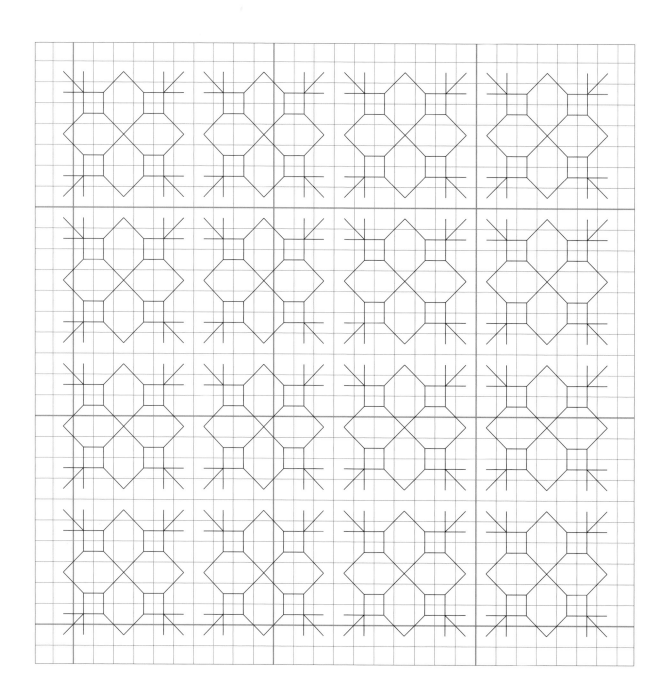

COLOUR KEY:

Blackwork cushion 2

━━━━━━━ ....DMC 310

VARIATIONS

The pattern on cushion 2 can be extended and worked as a stool top or chest top.

Blackwork sampler

This is a fairly easy piece to embroider, but do count the fabric threads carefully to ensure correct placing of the stitches. The finished size will depend on how much fabric you leave showing around the edge of the stitches. With this project, I started at the top and worked down, following my chart.

MATERIALS

◆ *About ¹/₂ skein of DMC stranded cotton 310*
◆ *32tpi evenweave fabric*
◆ *Tapestry needle size 28*
◆ *Thin card*
◆ *Fabric glue*
◆ *Picture frame*
◆ *Paint or stain*

DESIGN SIZE:
Approx. 1³/₄ x 1¹/₄in
(45 x 32mm)

STITCH COUNT:
58 x 41

STITCH SIZE:
Each stitch over one thread
of fabric

NUMBER OF STRANDS:
1

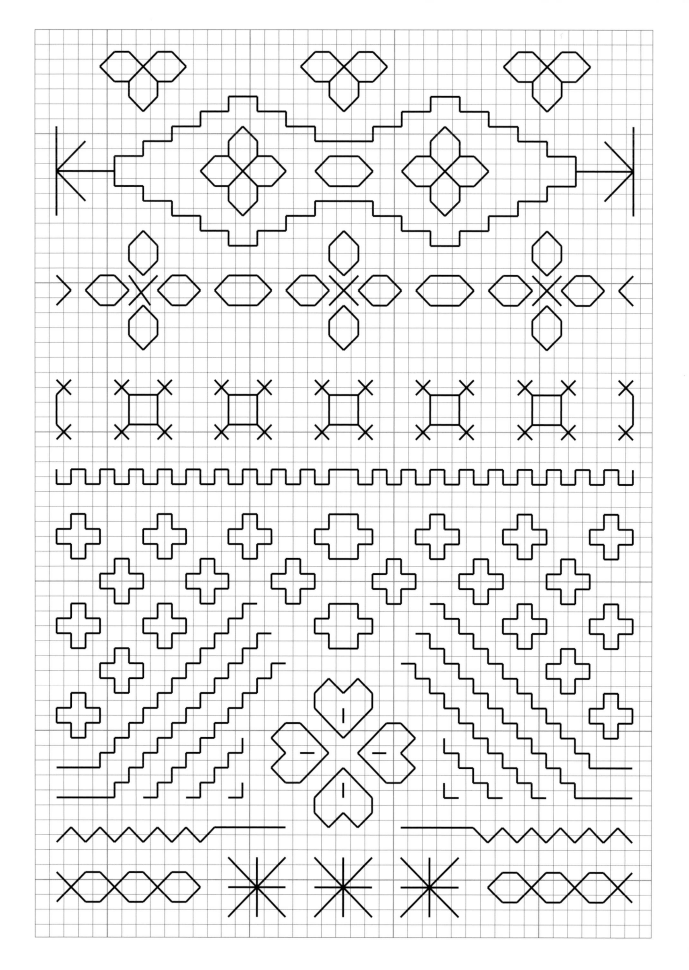

COLOUR KEY:
Blackwork sampler

━━━━━━━━ ....DMC 310

VARIATIONS

This design would look pretty worked in coloured thread for a cot cover or as a central design on a single bed cover. Try adding other motifs to make the design your own. (See 'Creating your own designs', pages 130–145.)

Blackwork bed cover

This elegant bedspread does not take long to embroider, as it is worked in backstitch, but do count very carefully between motifs; otherwise when you come to the last one you may find that they don't fit together as they should. I worked the top row of motifs first then one motif at either side. At this point I checked that they were level across the bed cover and continued working one on both sides and checking again until I reached the bottom row. Providing the top row is accurate, the bottom row should work out right.

Start with an Away Knot (see page 20) and finish your thread by weaving under the last few stitches and cutting close to the fabric. Take care to carry your thread between one motif and the next by weaving under worked stitches; this will ensure a neat back to the work.

MATERIALS

- ◆ About ¹/₂ skein of DMC stranded cotton 310
- ◆ 32tpi Belfast linen
- ◆ Embroidery needle size 10
- ◆ Fabric glue or sewing cotton

DESIGN SIZE:
Approx. 5¹/₂ x 3³/₄in
(140 x 95mm)

STITCH COUNT:
177 x 117

STITCH SIZE:
Each stitch over one thread
of fabric

NUMBER OF STRANDS:
1

COLOUR KEY:

Blackwork bed cover

■■■■■■ ....DMC 310

VARIATIONS

A row of tiny motifs can be worked along the edges of the bed cover. Try designing some on graph paper to make sure the corners look right. (See 'Creating your own designs', pages 130–145.) This bed cover would also look pretty worked in coloured threads – try experimenting on a spare piece of fabric.

Blackwork picture

I have chosen a very pale yellow fabric for this picture. It is not difficult to work, but care needs to be taken when counting the fabric threads to ensure that the pattern works out. Start with the tree and urn then work the railings and top trellis. I painted the frame a matt black.

MATERIALS

- *Small quantity of DMC stranded cotton 310*
- *28tpi pale yellow Permin linen*
- *Tapestry needle size 26*
- *Thin card*
- *Fabric glue*
- *Wooden picture frame*
- *Paint or stain*

DESIGN SIZE:
2 x 1¼in (50 x 32mm)

STITCH COUNT:
55 x 35

STITCH SIZE:
Each stitch over one thread of fabric

NUMBER OF STRANDS:
1

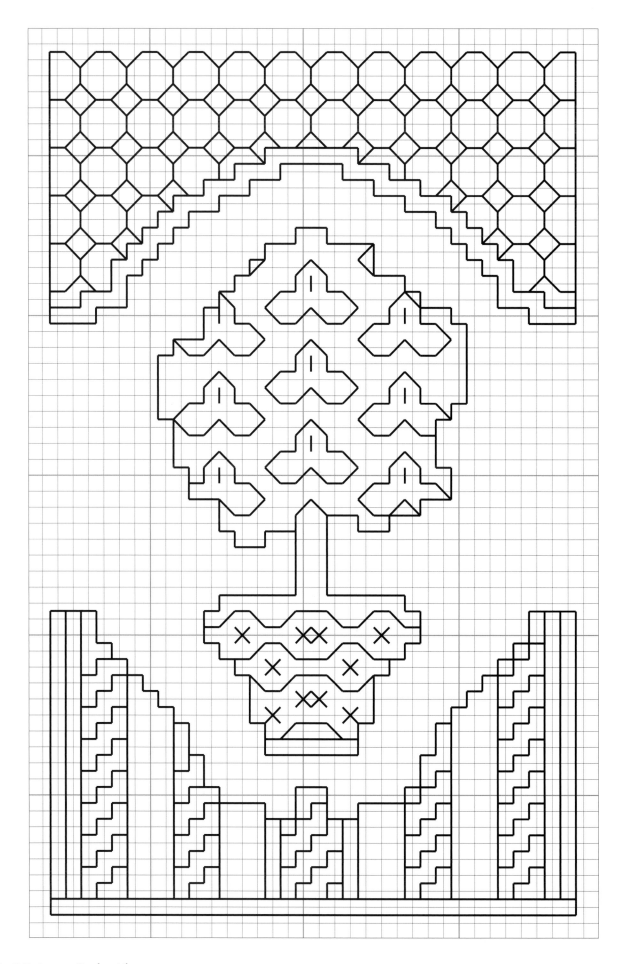

COLOUR KEY:

Blackwork picture

━━━━━━━━ ....DMC 310

VARIATIONS

Try your own infill patterns, remembering that the closer the stitches, the blacker the embroidery will seem. Experiment first on graph paper to ensure that the pattern works. The tree can be altered in size a little to accommodate a different infill design.

Blackwork wall hanging

This wall hanging demonstrates the use of colours while embroidering the blackwork technique. I have chosen to use random-dyed silk threads to add interest to the pattern shapes. (See 'Threads', page 18.) Work the outline of the shapes first in backstitch, counting the fabric threads carefully then fill in with the patterns. Work the backstitch border last.

MATERIALS

◆ *Selection of random-dyed silk threads*
◆ *30tpi linen*
◆ *Embroidery needle size 10*

DESIGN SIZE:
Approx. 3³/₄ x 2¹/₂in
(95 x 63mm)

STITCH COUNT:
8113 x 80

STITCH SIZE:
Each stitch over one thread
of fabric

NUMBER OF STRANDS:
1

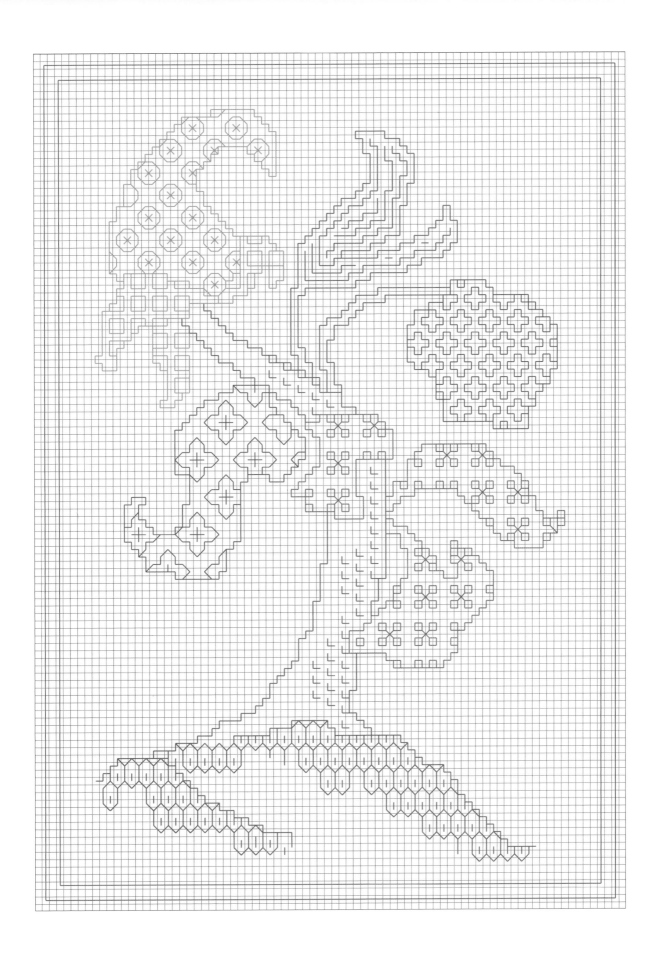

VARIATIONS

Using solid colour threads will alter the appearance of the wall hanging, and you may prefer this. You may also prefer a more elaborate border, in which case, plot the stitches first on graph paper to ensure that the corners work. (See 'Creating your own designs', pages 130–145.)

RUNNING STITCH

Another very simple stitch to work, but the effect can be delicate and pretty, as seen with the hall runner in this chapter. Running stitch is worked by weaving your needle in and out along the fabric, making several stitches before pulling the thread through. However, when working on a small, tautly framed piece of fabric, I find that using a stabbing action for each stitch is easier. But either way, the effect is the same: a row of evenly placed stitches of the same length with the same size of gap between each of them. (The gaps can be a different length to the stitches, but in miniature embroidery I think that gaps the same size as the stitches look better.)

Bring your needle up at the odd numbers and down at the even numbers. As with any straight stitch, do not pull your thread too tightly or it will disappear between the fabric threads; instead, simply let your stitches lie on top of the fabric.

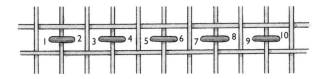

Close-up of running stitch

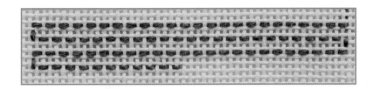

Running stitch – keep the tension of your
stitches as even as possible.

To complete
the project see
'Making up',
pages 148–151.

Hall runner

The central pattern on this runner is worked in backstitch and the two-row border in running stitch. Although the design is simple, by using random-dyed threads, the effect is attractive and unique. To avoid the need to work the background (which I think would spoil the effect), I have painted my fabric with two coats of fabric paint, but coloured linen could be used instead.

MATERIALS

◆ *Small quantity of random-dyed silk thread*

35tpi linen

◆ *Embroidery needle size 10*

◆ *Yellow fabric paint*

◆ *Fabric glue*

DESIGN SIZE:
Approx. $5^{3}/_{4}$ x $1^{1}/_{8}$in
(145 x 30mm)

STITCH COUNT:
195 x 41

STITCH SIZE:
Each stitch over one thread
of fabric

NUMBER OF STRANDS:
1

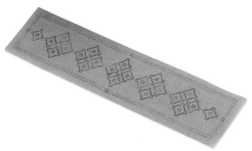

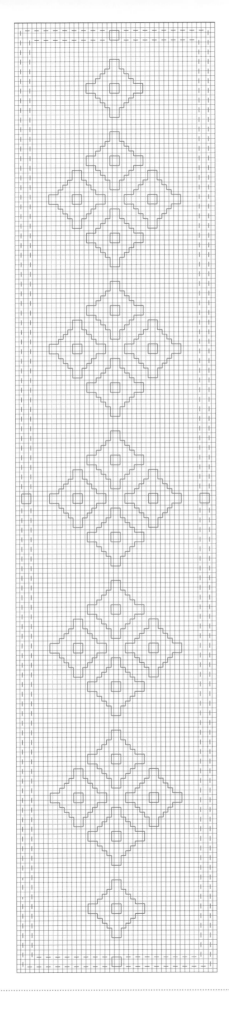

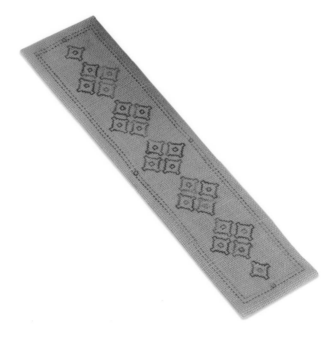

VARIATIONS

The central motifs can be used for other items, such as cushions and chair seats. Try also embroidering the runner in solid colours for an entirely different look.

UPRIGHT GOBELIN STITCH

This stitch probably doesn't have many uses for dolls' house embroidery, but it is quick and easy to work and can look dramatic. It is best used for flat items, such as rugs or wall hangings, as the fabric will show between the long stitches if it is curved over items such as chair seats or chest tops.

In full-size embroidery, stitches can be made over any number of threads, but in miniature work over three threads is enough to avoid a loopy, out-of-scale look. Bring your needle up at the odd numbers and down at the even numbers.

Close-up of upright Gobelin stitch

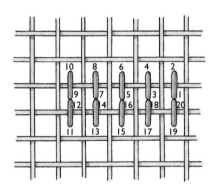

Upright Gobelin stitch

To complete
the project see
'Making up',
pages 148–151.

Striped rug

Gobelin stitch covers the fabric quickly, and this design is easily worked. Start with the salmon-coloured row that runs from top left to bottom right and work all other rows above and below, remembering to stop at the edges!

MATERIALS

◆ *1 skein of DMC stranded cotton 352, 472 and 732*

◆ *24tpi coin net*

◆ *Tapestry needle size 24*

◆ *Thin matching material for edging*

◆ *Fabric glue*

DESIGN SIZE:
Approx. 3 x 2in (76 x 50mm)

STITCH COUNT:
72 x 50

STITCH SIZE:
Each stitch over three thread of fabric

NUMBER OF STRANDS:
4

COLOUR KEY:

Striped rug

........DMC 352

........DMC 472

........DMC 732

VARIATIONS

The rug can be extended to make a larger carpet,
and you can work the design in colours to
complement your dolls' house furnishings.

FLORENTINE STITCH

I love embroidering this stitch. It is relatively quick to work, and once the first horizontal row has been worked, all others follow it, making it less necessary to keep referring to a chart.

Colour is everything in Florentine embroidery, and often three shades of one colour and two of another are combined, as with the mauve and green stool top that is on page 122. The peaks can be pointed or rounded and as dramatic as you like within the space that you have.

I have shown two charts for each project, one with lines and the other with blocks of colour, which you may find easier to follow. Try to work a dark-coloured row first, right across the design, and check it carefully to ensure it is correct. Then work the zigzags above and below, each time finishing a row before moving on to the next. When you are close to the top or bottom of the design, make sure you don't get carried away and take the zigzags further than they are meant to go. You will see from the charts that the top and bottom stitches may be over only one or two fabric threads. Designing your own Florentine pattern is very simple. For advice, see 'Creating your own designs', pages 130–145.

TIP Make sure that you use enough strands of threads in your needle so that the fabric does not show and spoil the vibrant effect of Florentine embroidery.

In these projects, the stitches are over either two or three threads, vertically, which is fine for miniature work. (In full-size embroidery, the stitches are usually worked over a larger number of threads.) Bring your needle up at the odd numbers and down at the even numbers.

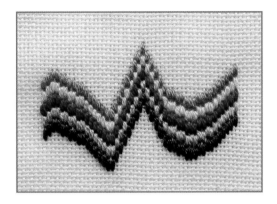

Close-up of Florentine stitch

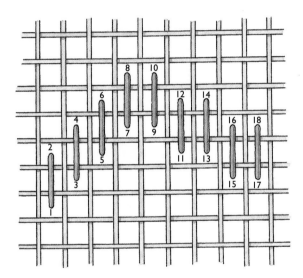

Florentine stitch worked vertically over two threads

To complete
each project see
'Making up',
pages 148–151.

Blue & brown cushion

Embroidered on 25tpi fabric, this cushion is quicker to work than the red and green cushion on page 128, but the effect is still good. Start with the brown row near the top and work right across it, then work all the lower rows and finally the odd part rows at the top. I have used a single six-strand length of thread as a trim.

MATERIALS

◆ *Small quantity of DMC stranded cotton*
  224, 798, 3722, 3823 and 3841
◆ *25tpi evenweave fabric*
◆ *Tapestry needle size 24 or 26*
◆ *Backing fabric*
◆ *Soft stuffing*

DESIGN SIZE:
Approx. 1¹⁄₈in (30mm) square

STITCH COUNT:
30 x 30

STITCH SIZE:
Each stitch over two threads
of fabric

NUMBER OF STRANDS:
3

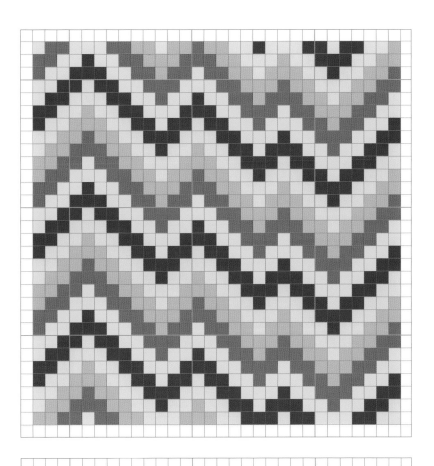

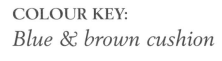

........DMC 224

........DMC 798

........DMC 3823

........DMC 3841

........DMC 3722

VARIATIONS

Try embroidering this simple design in different colour combinations to make a pretty set of cushions. Alternatively, design your own zigzag pattern. (See 'Creating your own designs', pages 130–145.)

Mauve & green stool

I have chosen a high-count fabric for this stool top, so that a lot of design can be worked in a relatively small space. However, because each stitch is worked over three threads, you will find that it will grow quickly. Once the first row is complete, the rest will follow easily without the need to keep referring to the chart.

MATERIALS

◆ About ¹/₂ skein of DMC stranded cotton 553, 563, 718, 3608 and 3814
◆ 38tpi silk gauze
◆ Embroidery needle size 10
◆ Thin card
◆ Fabric glue
◆ Stool base
◆ Wadding
◆ Decorative trim
◆ Paint or stain

DESIGN SIZE:
Approx. 1³/₄ x 1¹/₈in
(45 x 30mm)

STITCH COUNT:
60 x 38

STITCH SIZE:
Each stitch over three threads
of gauze

NUMBER OF STRANDS:
2

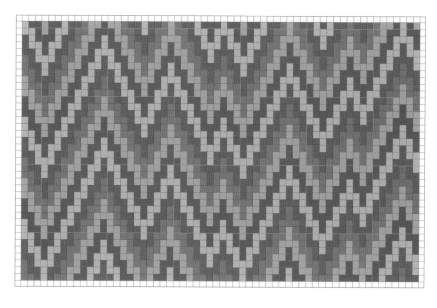

COLOUR KEY:

Mauve & green stool

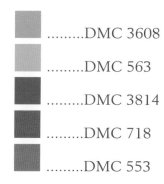

.........DMC 3608

.........DMC 563

.........DMC 3814

.........DMC 718

.........DMC 553

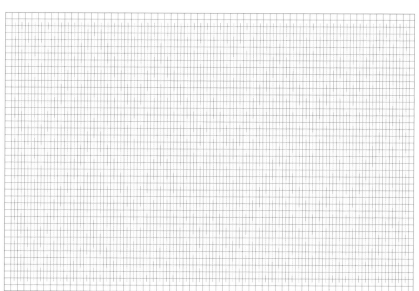

VARIATIONS

Stop working the zigzags about two thirds of the way along the length of the design (draw a line on the graph where you want to stop) and use the smaller-sized embroidery as a square cushion. For a larger cushion, use 27tpi cotton fabric.

Wall hanging

This is a more complex Florentine pattern than the stool top, but it is not too difficult to work. It resembles a tapestry, and it would be suitable to hang over a bed in a dark-wood panelled room in a dolls' house.

Embroider the red first, followed by the small zigzags of yellow, then the blue, green and dark grey, and lastly the single yellow stitches above the grey. You will see from the chart that while most stitches are over three fabric threads, some are over only one or two, but once you get the pattern going it's easy.

MATERIALS

◆ About ¹/₂ skein of DMC stranded cotton 413, 522, 834, 931 and 3722

◆ 24tpi coin net

◆ Tapestry needle size 24

◆ Non-fraying material for loops

◆ Fabric glue

DESIGN SIZE:
Approx. 2³/₄ x 2³/₈in
(70 x 60mm)

STITCH COUNT:
67 x 57

STITCH SIZE:
Most stitches over three threads of fabric, others over 1 or 2

NUMBER OF STRANDS:
4

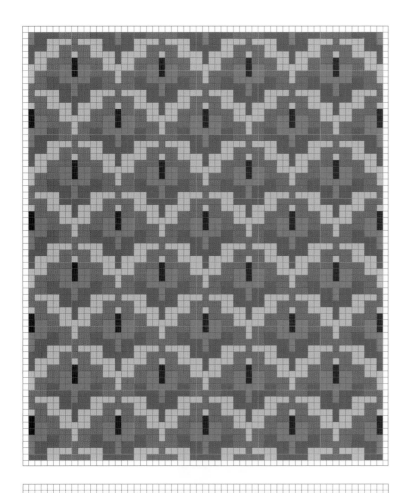

.........DMC 834

.........DMC 3722

.........DMC 522

.........DMC 413

.........DMC 931

VARIATIONS

I think this design would make a very pretty long stool top. Just start and stop the pattern to fit a stool, trying to keep the balance of pattern central to the stool top and allowing a little extra for the padding. Use a softer fabric, such as a 25tpi Lugana cotton.

Green & brown stool

'Mirror image' patterns like this take a little while to design, and the chart needs to be followed carefully, but I think the effect in miniature embroidery is worth the effort. Start with the central pink and brown stitches and carefully work around these in one colour at a time. The pattern can be extended to fit your stool by keeping the full rows going, but don't forget to eventually stop working the pattern at the corners or else your stool top will grow and grow…

MATERIALS

- About ¹/₂ skein of DMC stranded cotton Ecru, 501, 778, 3817 and 3772
- 32tpi evenweave fabric
- Tapestry needle size 28
- Thin card
- Fabric glue
- Stool base
- Paint or stain
- Trim

DESIGN SIZE:
Approx. 1⁵/₈ x 1¹/₈in
(40 x 30mm)

STITCH COUNT:
51 x 38

STITCH SIZE:
Each stitch over two threads
of fabric

NUMBER OF STRANDS:
2

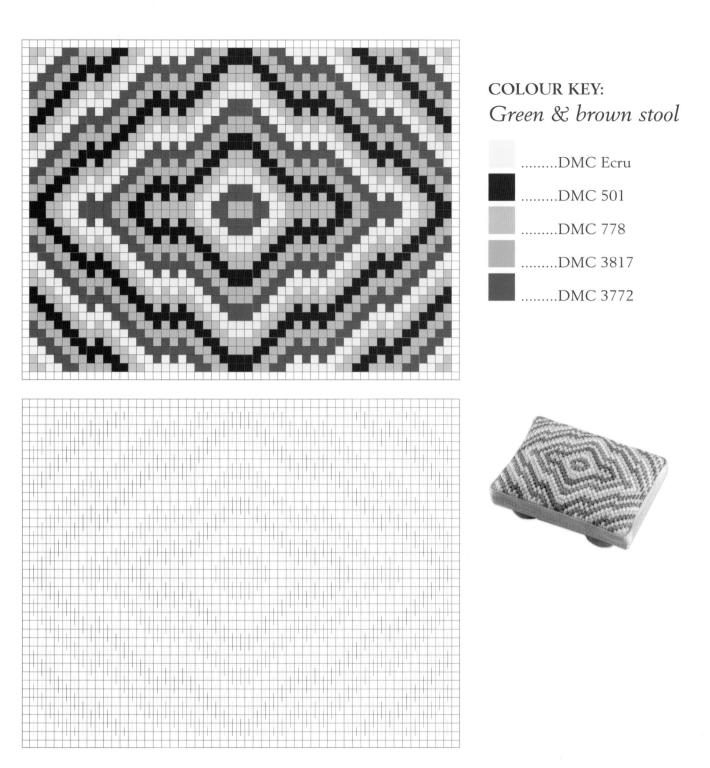

COLOUR KEY:
Green & brown stool

⬜	........DMC Ecru
⬛	........DMC 501
🟩	........DMC 778
🟩	........DMC 3817
🟫	........DMC 3772

VARIATIONS

This design can be worked as smart rectangular cushions or worked on a lower-count fabric for a small rug. I suggest using an 18tpi canvas for a rug, with as many strands of thread in your needle as necessary to cover the fabric. This will depend partly on the colours you choose. (Florentine and other straight stitches require more thickness of thread than stitches that cross the fabric.) Your rug will be approximately 3 x 2in (76 x 50mm). You may then like to put fringes at both ends.

Red & green cushion

This smart cushion could grace a sofa in the drawing room of any dolls' house. Worked on 40tpi silk gauze, the stitching looks perfectly 'in scale' and I feel my effort at working on a fairly high fabric count is well rewarded. (One day I'll make a matching set!)

Start with the dark green zigzag near the top and work it right across. Then continue working every row below and, finally, above. Like all Florentine embroidery, your work will grow quickly. I have used a single strand of thread to edge the cushion.

MATERIALS

◆ *1/2 skein of DMC stranded cotton 223, 501, 523, 819 and 355*

◆ *40tpi silk gauze*

◆ *Embroidery or quilting needle size 10*

◆ *Backing fabric*

◆ *Soft stuffing*

◆ *Trimming*

DESIGN SIZE:
Approx. 1¼in (32mm) square

STITCH COUNT:
52 x 48

STITCH SIZE:
Each stitch over three threads of gauze

NUMBER OF STRANDS:
2

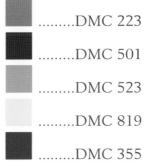

COLOUR KEY:
Red & green cushion

■ ....DMC 223

■ ....DMC 501

■ ....DMC 523

□ ....DMC 819

■ ....DMC 355

VARIATIONS

If 40tpi silk gauze is difficult for you to work with, the cushion will still be in scale if the design is worked on 27tpi Linda cotton. For this you will need to use at least three strands of thread in your needle; the finished size will then be approximately 2 x 1¾in (50 x 45mm).

CREATING YOUR OWN DESIGNS

DESIGNING CHARTS

Following a published chart is how most embroiders start, and for many it is their preferred method of working. However, if you wish to create something unique, you will need to design your own chart. This adds an extra dimension to the enjoyment of miniature embroidery, and is not difficult to do. Indeed, the simplest of designs are often the most effective.

What do I need?

Graph paper, pencil, eraser and coloured pencils.

The materials and equipment that you will need

Do I need to be good at drawing?

No, start with a fairly simple shape and repeat it, perhaps mirror fashion, until a design appears.

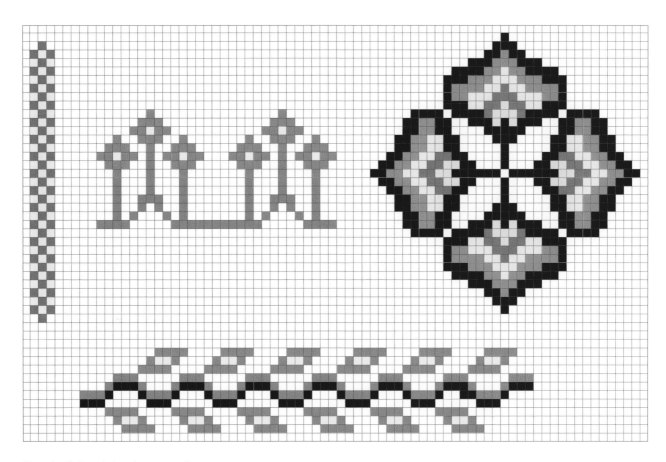

Example of chart designs for tent stitch, cross stitch or half-cross stitch

For tent stitch, cross stitch or half-cross stitch, colour in the squares on your paper, each square to represent one stitch. Experiment with pattern shapes, trying variations such as simple floral shapes and symmetrical repetitive patterns. Colour in lots of samples of patterns and see whether some, or all, can be incorporated into a project. Then try designing a border (see page 137). It really is as simple as sitting down with coloured pencils and graph paper and taking a little time. When you are pleased with your design, start the embroidery, and when complete you will have a unique piece of work for your dolls' house.

For straight stitches, such as backstitch, Florentine or Gobelin stitch, draw straight lines between the graph lines, to represent the stitches. (See How to read charts, pages 33–35.)

Blackwork is usually a simple mix of backstitch and cross stitch, the effect of light and dark being achieved by varying the density of the stitching. Your design can be as simple or as complex as you wish.

Often, very simple shapes, when repeated, create interesting designs. You can combine these, perhaps in rows, to make a sampler.

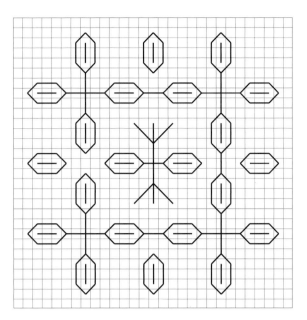

Example of chart design for blackwork

embroidery, it is best not to take each stitch over more than three vertical fabric threads. For more complex designs, such as the green and brown stool on page 126, it helps to divide the pattern area into four and draw the lines in one quarter, then use tracing paper to turn the design around the other three corners. With all designs, try different colour combinations until you find one that you are really happy with.

To design for infilled blackwork, having decided on the finished stitch count of your motif (see 'Calculating size', pages 139–140), draw this shape onto graph paper, each line on the paper representing a thread of fabric and then try different infill patterns until you find one that pleases you. Spend time drawing different designs on graph paper and then try embroidering them on a spare piece of your chosen fabric to see how they look. There are many blackwork design books available that are published for full-size embroidery; these should provide plenty of inspiration.

Designing for Gobelin stitch is really all about colour, as the stitches are upright and of the same length, usually in straight or diagonal rows. To design a simple pattern using Florentine stitch, draw a zigzag on graph paper, either with sharp peaks, rounded peaks or a combination of both, and 'square it off', as shown, ensuring that all stitches in a row are the same length vertically. Use coloured pencils to draw where the stitches will be, following the original shape. For miniature

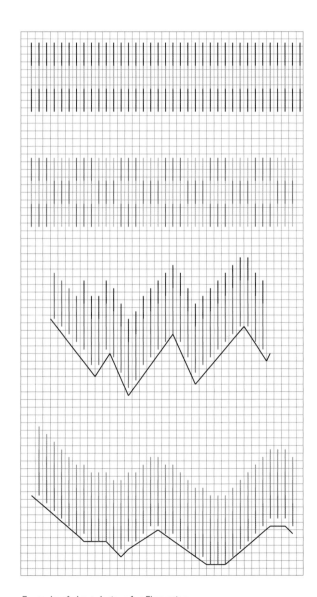

Example of chart designs for Florentine and Gobelin stitches

Where can I take design inspiration?

Design ideas are all around us. Take inspiration from furnishing fabrics, wrapping paper, wallpapers and the such-like. Keep swatches of fabric or paper if you like the design on them.

Fabrics and papers can provide design inspiration

 ## *Why design for myself instead of following a printed chart?*

You may need something specific, either for your dolls' house or that of a friend, or you may just be unable to find a design that you really want to work. The finished piece will be unique.

 ## *How do I start?*

Decide on the finished size of the item you are to design and what fabric count you are happy with. Calculate the number of stitches across and down (see 'Calculating size', pages 139–140) and draw this shape on graph paper (each square = one stitch over one thread of fabric). Begin to plot your design using coloured pencils.

What makes a good design?

Beauty, it is said, is in the eye of the beholder; therefore various designs will appeal to different people. However, there are a few 'rules' that help.

Balance *– try to keep heavier motifs below centre, so that the design does not look top heavy.*

Motifs *– distribute them evenly. Any design that needs to face in a particular direction will look better facing towards the centre if possible, i.e. trains, people, animals, even sprigs of flowers.*

Ease of working *– limit the number of colours where you can. Make sure you are happy with the design on paper before you start embroidering. Ask yourself, does the balance of pattern look right for the finished size? Is there too much (or too little) border pattern? Is the design unnecessarily fussy, therefore making it harder to work? Can the number of colours be reduced while still achieving your desired result?*

How important is colour?

Never underestimate the importance of colour. A first opinion on an item is often made by colour alone. (See 'Choosing colours', pages 141–145, for guidelines.)

Will I need to choose my colours before I start embroidering?

Not necessarily. It is useful (and perhaps safer) to have an idea of colour before you start, but if you feel confident, just let the colours come to you as you work.

Can I start embroidering without first drawing a chart?

Yes. It is your design, so if you are confident of what you want to achieve, go ahead. However, it is important to have an idea of the finished size to avoid the piece being out of scale, and most people find it easier to have at least a few details on graph paper. Remember, it is much easier to erase marks on paper than it is to undo miniature stitches!

Can I alter the chart as I go along and, if so, is there anything I should take care with?

Yes, by all means alter the chart as you work, but be aware that this can have an effect elsewhere in the design, particularly with borders.

How can I create a border with corners that 'work'?

Borders are by no means essential, but they can work well to hold a design together. They can simply be one or more straight lines of colour, but for more elaborate designs, always plot them first on graph paper to ensure that the corners 'work'.

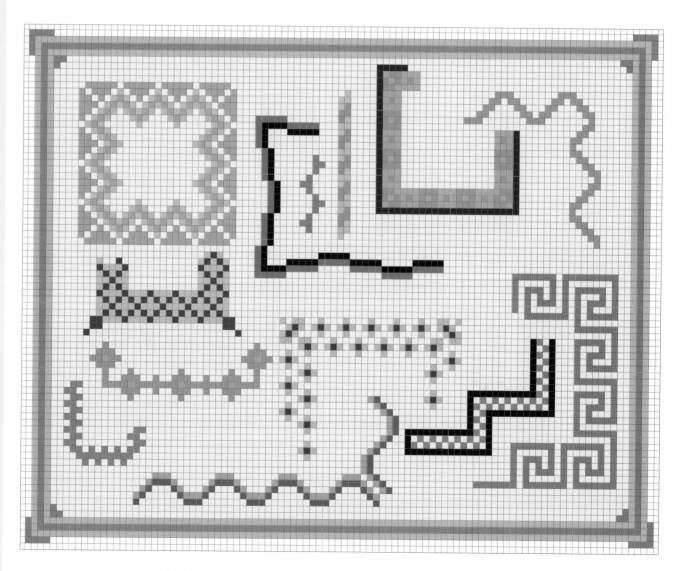

Border pattern examples

Start from the central position of your design, along the top edge, drawing your chosen shape in both directions until you reach the corners. Do the same along the bottom edge and then both sides. You may be lucky enough to find the pattern meets neatly at the corners. However, this is often not the case, and you need to decide on one of the options available to you.

It may be necessary to extend your border area outwards or bring it in a little towards the main pattern area. This alters the number of stitches along the top, bottom and sides of the border and can help in creating pleasing corners. Alternatively, you can treat the corners separately by giving them a slightly different pattern shape from the main border. Another option is to accept that the best way to solve the problem is to have alternate corners matching each other.

Where the pattern really cannot be taken around the corner, draw a diagonal line in from the corner and create a mirror image of the pattern on either side of the line, then continue to the next corner and repeat. This can look quite clever, but is actually very simple. Whichever way you choose, remember to keep your main pattern central to the border.

 ## Is it necessary to plot letters and numbers before working?

Yes, unless you are very used to working them. Many letters and numbers require a minimum of five stitches to make them work, and by drawing them first on graph paper you will be able to estimate the area that they need.

 ## Are there computer programs to help me?

There are computer programs on the market specifically designed to help with creating your own patterns, and, once mastered, they are invaluable. They carry popular thread manufacturers' colour charts and thousands of motifs covering hundreds of categories. (The motifs are usually copyrighted, so cannot be used if you intend to sell or publish your work.) It is possible to view your design enlarged or greatly reduced in size (very useful for miniature work) and the program will calculate how much thread is needed to work it. Many have the facility for scanning in your own pictures or photographs to convert to embroidery.

 ## Is it useful to keep all my efforts at designing?

Yes, even those that you don't like now or those where the corners just won't 'work'. They will be a visual record of how your designing is progressing and will also provide inspiration as a starting point for a new design.

CALCULATING SIZE

If you are following a printed chart, it will almost certainly state the finished dimensions. However, when creating your own design, it is important to be able to calculate the finished size before you start. This will avoid oversized (or undersized) chair seats, cushions, and so on. Simple mathematics is all that is required.

How do I know from the chart what size my embroidery will be?

Count the number of squares across and down the chart and count the number of threads to the inch on your chosen fabric. Let us say that the chart has 120 squares across and 80 down, and that your fabric is 20 threads to the inch (25mm). Divide this 20 into 120 = 6 and divide 20 into 80 = 4. So your finished embroidery will be 6 x 4in (150 x 100mm).

How can I alter the size of the finished item without altering the chart?

By using a different count of fabric to the one suggested on the chart. To make the finished piece larger, use a lower number of threads to the inch (25mm) fabric and to make it smaller, use a higher number of threads to the inch (25mm). Remember, it is the fabric count that decides the finished size of your embroidery, not the chart.

Will some measurements work for either 1/12 or 1/24 scale dolls' houses?

Yes. For example, a 1in (25mm) square cushion will be a small cushion for 1/12 scale house and larger (but perfectly in scale) for a 1/24 scale house. A small rug in a 1/12 scale house will become a carpet in a 1/24 house, and items such as pictures or wall hangings will often work for both scales.

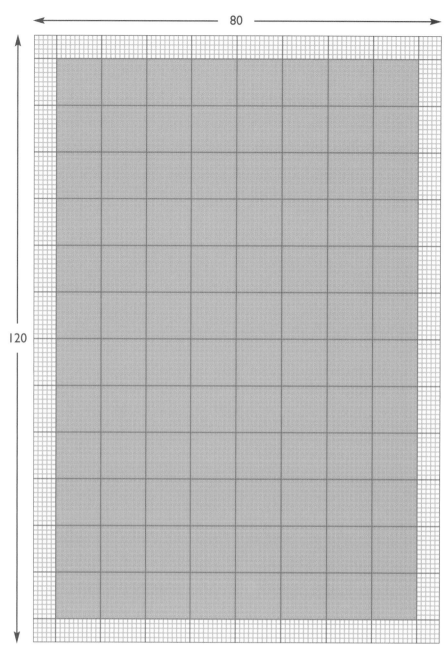

Graph showing a chart with
120 stitches x 80 stitches

Fabric: 20 threads to the inch (25mm)
Divide the number of squares by 20:
$120 \div 20 = 6$
$80 \div 20 = 4$
Finished size of embroidery 6 x 4in (150 x 100mm)

 ## *How much extra fabric should I allow around the edges of my work?*

Allow enough to attach to a frame. (See 'Frames', pages 23–25.) Use masking tape to bind the edges if fraying could be a problem. Remember also that you will need to leave some unworked fabric around the edges for possible blocking (see 'Blocking', pages 39–41) and making up (see 'Making up', pages 148–151).

CHOOSING COLOURS

Colour is often the first thing to attract us to an item, so time spent choosing the right combination of colours should ensure that you are pleased with the finished result.

When furnishing a dolls' house, you may like to choose colours that were used during the period in which you have set the house, or perhaps choose dark, fairly muted colours for an 'antique' look. Clear, bright colours will give you a modern, contemporary look. Keep a scrapbook and fill it with scraps of fabric or pictures that have appealed to you for their colour combinations. You will find this very useful when you need inspiration for the colours of a new project.

It is also important to remember that the texture of a stitch can affect the shade of a colour. Tent stitch makes a colour slightly darker, while a raised stitch, such as Rhodes, will catch the light and make the thread appear lighter. Threads with a silky sheen will appear lighter than the same shade of wool. Take the time to work a small test piece before you begin your project. You will then be able to see whether you need to alter the shade of one or two of your colours.

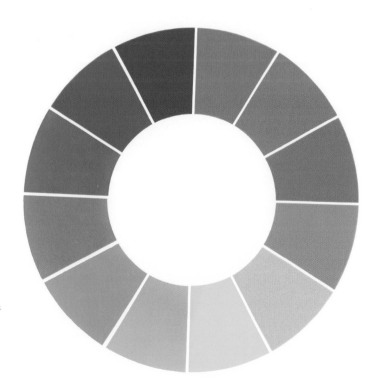

A colour wheel is a useful reference chart for seeing which colour combinations you like

TIP Some colours cover fabric better than others. For example, if you are using a dark colour on a light-coloured fabric, you may need more strands of thread in your needle.

 Where can I find inspiration to help me combine colours?

Colour is all around us, and we can take inspiration from fabrics, clothes, wrapping paper, wallpaper, magazines, and so on. Try also rearranging the little blocks of colour on paint manufacturers' charts and matching your threads to a combination that you like.

Paint charts often have colour blocks shown under different titles, such as Georgian, Victorian, Contemporary, and this can be very useful if you are seeking a period look in your dolls' house.

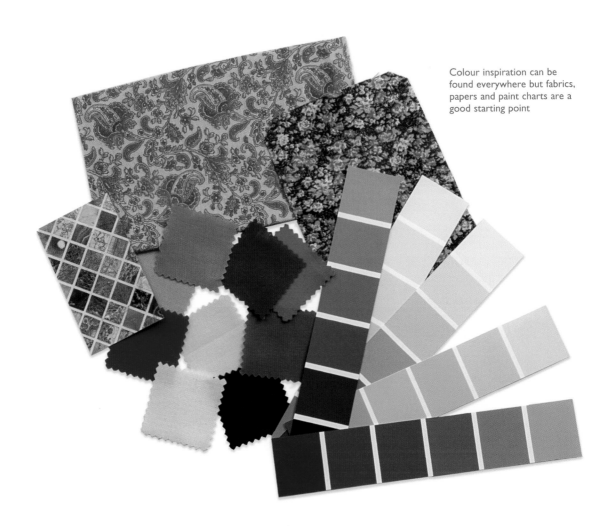

Colour inspiration can be found everywhere but fabrics, papers and paint charts are a good starting point

Can I use colours that are very similar to each other?

Items that have been embroidered for a dolls' house are very small and, unfortunately, colours that are too similar will not appear distinguishable from each other. Instead, the tiny pattern shapes that you have so carefully worked will merge into one another, giving an all over 'grey' appearance to the work. It is therefore important to choose colours that are sufficiently different, so that even if the pattern requires you to work just one stitch in a different colour from its surrounding stitches, the difference will show. Always work a small piece using your chosen fabric and threads to make sure that the colours 'work'.

How will I know whether the colours will look how I imagine them?

Hold your skeins of thread together in a good light (daylight if possible) and decide whether the combination is pleasing. Does one colour 'jump out' from the others or is the whole look just too boring? Keep adding to or removing skeins of thread until you are really satisfied with those you have chosen. Don't be afraid to be a little bold sometimes; often the best designs have small amounts of really bright colours that bring life to the whole piece. Work a few stitches of each colour on your chosen fabric and see how they relate to each other. Colours will look different against other colours. For example, a navy blue will look very dark against a pale lemon and less dark (but quite dramatic) against a deep red.

Is there a way to know the effects of different colour combinations?

Yes. We all know that reds, oranges and yellows are regarded as 'hot' colours and navy, blues and aquamarines are known as 'cool' colours. It is also helpful to refer to a colour wheel. Colours taken from opposite sides of the wheel will complement each other, three colours equal distance apart will provide an exciting, striking look, and by using colours from just one third of the colour wheel, you will achieve a relaxing, easy-on-the-eye effect.

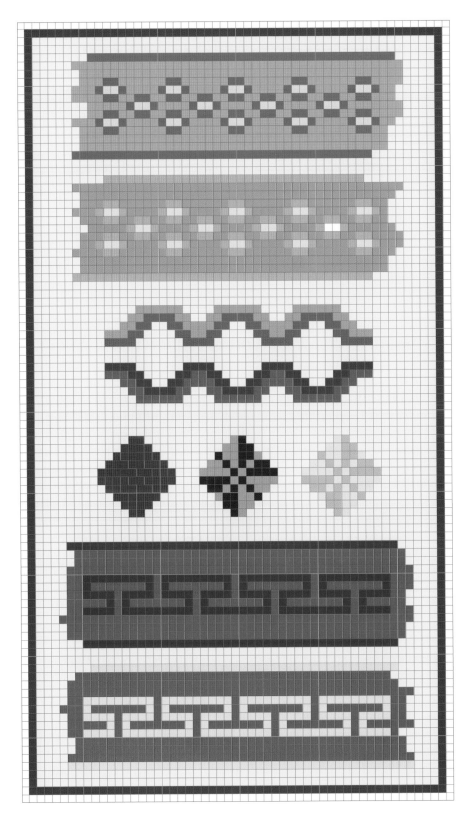

Colour chart showing designs worked
in different colour combinations

Can I mix colours in my needle?

Yes. This technique works as well for miniature embroidery as it does for full-size work and can, for example, create an illusion of shadow if a dark colour is added to a colour you have already used. But there are a few points to watch out for. Lay the colours side by side and thread them together through the eye of the needle and, as you work, try to ensure that they do not become twisted. (To avoid this, let your needle drop occasionally to untwist the thread.) When using two or more colours together, the overall look tends to be a little darker, and you will need to work a practice piece on a spare scrap of fabric to ensure the look is what you want. Mixing the right colours in your needle can help you to achieve a worn appearance to a carpet or just take away the 'too new' look of a piece. This is ideal if you want an antique look in a dolls' house. When using random-dyed threads, unless you want a speckled look, use lengths with the same colour shading.

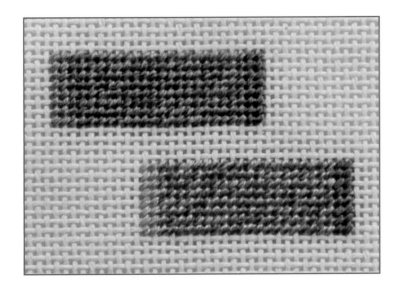

Examples of embroidery that have been worked with two colours of thread in the needle

 ## Does it matter how many colours I use for one piece of embroidery?

No, but often the best designs have a limited number of colours. I find that five colours can work well, but do experiment and use three (or thirty!) if that achieves the look you want.

THE FINAL
STAGE

MAKING UP

It is probably true to say that few people actually enjoy the making up process of miniature embroidery, but there is certainly some satisfaction in finishing an item as professionally as possible. I often wait until I have completed several projects and make them all up at the same time.

Firstly, remove your embroidery from the frame and, if necessary, pull gently into shape. If it is badly distorted, you may need to block it (see 'Blocking', pages 39–41). If you wish, the embroidery can be placed face down on a clean soft cloth and pressed gently with a warm iron. There are many ways of making up items for the dolls' house. The following are a sample of the ones I use most frequently.

Cushions

Trim the fabric, leaving a margin of approximately five holes, and cut a matching or contrasting piece of backing fabric the same overall size. (Use thin material for this, and preferably one that does not fray too much. Cotton lawn and silk work well.)

Turn under the four edges of your embroidered fabric so that the outside stitches lie along the edges then crease with your fingers and thumbs. Crease over the edges of the backing fabric so that it is the same size. If you wish, cut away a little of the excess fabric at the corners. Place the wrong sides together and oversew using a matching thread and fine needle, keeping the stitches as small as possible. Leave an opening along the bottom edge.

TIP Keep the cushion as 'square' as possible. Sometimes it helps to pin the two fabrics together, using a fine lace pin, while you sew.

If you prefer, sew the two fabric pieces right sides together, but take great care when you turn them out to the right side, as both are liable to fray.

Tease a small amount of soft stuffing into tiny wisps and carefully fill the cushion, making sure that the filling goes right into the corners. Cushions look more natural if they are not overfilled. Sew the remaining edges together. (Tiny beads also make a good filling for cushions.)

Providing your oversewing does not show, the edges of your cushion can be left plain. Alternatively, decorate them with very narrow braid, ribbon, wool or plaited stranded cotton. To attach the trimming, either couch using matching or contrasting thread or apply a very small amount of fabric glue to the cushion edges and stick in place, allowing one edge at a time to dry before doing the next and overlapping slightly at the ends.

Stools and chest tops

If your stool or chest already has a covered top, carefully remove the top padded part. Either cover this with your embroidery or, if this is too bulky, make a thin card template that fits the top and stick a little soft wadding onto it.

Wrap your embroidery around it and use fabric glue to stick the turned-over edges onto the card. Remove some of the excess fabric at the corners if necessary. Leave to dry and then stick to your stool or chest. Use fabric glue to attach thin ribbon or braid, etc. to the edges, overlapping a little where they meet.

Rugs and carpets

OVERSEWN EDGES:
Turn the edges over so that the next row of holes runs along the edges. Using at least one extra strand of thread in your needle, begin oversewing, using the same holes that your last stitches occupied and ensuring that your oversewing stitches all lie vertically through both layers of fabric.

It is easier to start a little way in from one of the corners and when each corner is reached, mitre the fabric or canvas, making the join as neat and flat as possible. Do not pull the thread too tightly and ensure that the corners are well covered. When complete, a little fabric glue can be applied under the turned-down edges, if desired.

STUCK DOWN EDGES:
Turn under the four sides, mitring the corners. (It is important to turn the canvas or fabric over sufficiently, so that the unworked areas cannot be seen from the front.) Apply a little fabric glue and stick down one edge at a time.

If you would like to add a fringe to your rug, you will need a piece of plain thin material to match one of the colours you have used. Cut two pieces, each a little longer than the ends of your rug and about ³/₄in (20mm) wide. Carefully fray this to whatever length you require by pulling out the cross threads one at a time. Use fabric glue to stick the unfrayed parts to the underside of your rug. Trim if necessary. If the material is very thin, put two layers together for a fuller look.

Fire screens

Paint or stain your frame if necessary. Most commercially bought fire screens rely on the embroidery being applied straight onto the front, and some have a narrow wooden trim to place over the embroidery edges to neaten. Alternatively, you can cut a thin piece of card to exactly fit the fire screen and apply a thin layer of glue to it, scraping off any excess with a spare piece of card. Do not trim your embroidery fabric but lay it centrally on the card and press gently to stick. (It helps to hold the card up to the light, so that you can make sure your embroidery is straight.) Allow to dry then cut away the excess fabric so that it exactly fits the card. Apply a little glue to the fire screen and stick the card onto it.

Wall hangings, bell-pulls and runners

Making up these items is blissfully simple but, as always, care should be taken to get the finish as professional as possible, with neat square corners. Fold the excess fabric over, fairly close to the embroidery. (The exact amount of unworked fabric you have showing on the front is a matter of choice, depending on the size you want the item to be.) Crease these folds between your fingers and thumbs and cut away the excess fabric to leave a turning of about $1/4$in (6mm). Apply a small amount of fabric glue along the back of the side edges and stick down.

When dry, fold over the top and bottom edges and stick down. You should find you can achieve neat corners without mitring them, but they can be mitred if you prefer.

To make a simple bell-pull tassel, wind a length of thread several times around a narrow strip of card then carefully remove the card. Tie another piece of thread around the tassel near the top and cut and trim the bottom edges. Attach with a few stitches to the bottom edge of your work.

To make top loops for wall hangings, cut a length of spare embroidery fabric about $5/8$in (15mm) wide and about 4in (100mm) long, making sure that the grain is straight. Place a thin line of glue down the centre and fold over one long side, so that it is approximately two thirds in, then immediately fold the other side over until it is just short of the opposite edge. Press together with your fingers. When dry, cut short lengths and fold each in half lengthways, with the join on the inside, and space evenly along the top edge of the wall hanging. (Usually, three will be required.) Apply a small amount of glue to the bottom edge of each loop and press into position. When dry, push a small piece of dowelling or thin brass rod through the loops, allowing it to extend slightly beyond the wall hanging.

Frames, pictures and samplers

Commercially bought miniature picture frames are mostly inexpensive and come in all sizes with many different styles and finishes. Choose one that suits your embroidery and, if necessary, paint or stain it to get the finish that you want.

Do not trim your embroidery fabric but cut a piece of thin card to exactly fit the aperture of the frame. Apply a small amount of glue to the card, scraping away any excess, and carefully lay your embroidery centrally onto it. It helps to hold it up to the light to see if the fabric is straight with the card.

Press gently and allow to dry. Trim the excess fabric to exactly fit the card. Lay the frame face down and apply a little glue to the inner edge. Place your embroidery face down onto it and press gently.

Bed covers

If your bed cover just lies on top of the bed, trim to the finished size, allowing small turnings all around. Fold these turnings under and catch down with tiny stitches in a matching thread, or glue down with fabric glue. If you wish, hem a piece of thin backing fabric to the reverse side.

If your bed cover hangs down both sides of the bed, cut to the required size for your bed, leaving small turnings. Turn these under and hem with tiny stitches, mitring the corners.

Cot covers

Trim the embroidery fabric, allowing for small turnings all around. Fold these under and apply a little fabric glue to hold. To back the cot cover, cut a slightly larger piece of silky fabric in a matching or contrasting colour then press under the edges so that it is marginally smaller than the cover. Place the wrong sides together and hem, using a matching thread and very tiny stitches.

MAIL ORDER SUPPLIERS

AUSTRALIA

E-MU NEEDLEWORK SUPPLIES
250 CHURCH STREET
MUDGEE
NWS, AUSTRALIA
Tel: +61 (02) 6372 4166
Email: emu@winsoft.net.au
Web: e-mu.au.com
(Suppliers of fabrics, charts, materials, threads and accessories.)

CANADA

BONNIE'S CROSS-STITCH ZONE
P.O. BOX 3009
STN TERMINAL MPP
KAMLOOPS
BCV2C, CANADA
Canadian orders: 800 877 4230
International orders: +1 (250) 377 8662
Web: crossstitchzone.com
(Suppliers of patterns, fabrics, threads, accessories and kits.)

UK

DIXIE COLLECTION
PO BOX 575
BROMLEY
BR2 7WP, ENGLAND
Tel/fax +44 (0)20 8462 0700
Email: sales@dixiecollection.co.uk
Web: www.dixiecollection.co.uk
(Suppliers of dolls' house haberdashery and miniatures for dolls, dolls' house and craft projects.)

GET STITCHING
CAMELFORD, CORNWALL
PL32 9SG, ENGLAND
Tel/fax +44 (0)8452 262041
Email: sales@GetStitching.com
Web: www.GetStitching.com
(Suppliers of evenweave fabrics, needlecraft kits, charts and accessories.)

SIESTA
UNIT D
LONGMEADOW INDUSTRIAL ESTATE
THREE LEGGED CROSS
WIMBORNE, DORSET
BH21 6RD, ENGLAND
Tel/fax +44 (0)1202 813363
Web: www.siestaframes.com
(Suppliers of frames, scissors, magnifying lamps etc.)

SILKEN STRANDS
20 Y RHOS
BANGOR, GWYNEDD
LL57 2LT, WALES
Tel/Fax: +44 (0)1248 362361
Email: sales@silkenstrands.co.uk
(Suppliers of embroidery threads, fine wools and accessories.)

THE ORIGINAL DOLLS HOUSE COMPANY (DIJON) LTD
THE OLD PRINT WORKS
STREATFIELD ROAD, HEATHFIELD
TN21 8LA, ENGLAND
Tel +44 (0)1435 864155
Fax +44 (0)1453 865108
Email: info@dijon.co.uk
Web: www.dijon.co.uk
(Suppliers of dolls' houses, dolls' house furniture and accessories.)

WILLOW FABRICS
95 TOWN LANE
MOBBERLEY
KNUTSFORD, CHESHIRE
WA16 7HH, ENGLAND
Tel +44 (0)1565 872225
Fax +44 (0)1565 872239
Email: major@willow fabrics.com
Web: www.willowfabrics.com
(Suppliers of evenweave fabrics, canvas, needles, scissors and sundries.)

USA

STITCHES N' THINGS
723 N.STATE ROAD (M–15)
DAVISON, M14823
Tel: +1 (810) 653 6532
Fax: +1 (810) 653 3833
Email: deb@stitchesnthings.com
WebL www.stitchesnthings.com
(Suppliers of threads and accessories.)

VICTORIAN COTTAGE TREASURES
P.O. BOX 752
PORTHILL, ID USA
83853 0752
Tel: +1 (250) 428 9395
Fax: +1 (250) 428 9395
Web: www.victoriancottagetreasures.com
(Suppliers of classic and speciality embroidery products.)

THREAD CONVERSION CHART

This conversion chart is for guidance only, as exact comparisons are not always possible.

Anchor	DMC	Madeira	Anchor	DMC	Madeira	Anchor	DMC	Madeira	Anchor	DMC	Madeira
1	blanc	2401	162	825	1107	330	947	205			
6	353	2605	164	824	2505	332	946	207	894	3326	813
8	3824	304	185	964	1112	333	608	206	895	223	812
10	351	406	186	959	1113	334	606	209	896	315	810
13	347	211	188	943	2706	335	606	209	897	221	2606
19	817	407	189	991	2705	337	922	403	899	3022	1906
20	3777	2502	205	912	1213	341	355	314	903	3032	2002
22	815	2501	206	564	1210	343	932	1710	905	3021	1904
35	3705	411	214	368	2604	349	301	2306	968	778	808
38	3731	611	215	320	1310	351	400	2304	969	816	809
45	814	2606	216	367	1310	352	300	2304	970	3726	2609
46	6566	210	217	319	1312	357	975	2602	1012	948	305
47	304	510	227	701	1305	358	801	2008	1014	355	2502
49	3689	607	236	3799	1713	359	898	2007	1021	963	404
50	605	613	241	703	1307	360	938	2005	1023	760	405
52	957	2707	245	701	1305	368	436	2011	1024	3328	406
54	956	611	246	986	1404	369	435	2010	1025	347	407
68	3687	604	253	772	1604	371	433	2602	1027	223	812
69	3685	2609	254	3348	1409	372	738	2013	1036	336	1712
70	*	2608	255	907	1410	376	842	1910	1037	3756	2504
74	3354	606	256	906	1411	378	841	2601	1042	369	1701
75	3733	505	264	3348	1409	379	840	2601	1070	993	
76	961	505	265	471	1308	380	838	2005	1072	993	
78	600	2609	266	470	1502	382	3371	2004	1074	3814	
85	3609	710	267	469	1503	386	746	2512	1089	996	
94	917	706	268	937	1504	390	822	1908	1090	996	
97	554	711	269	895	1507	397	3204	1901	5975	356	401
99	552	2714	276	3770	2314	398	415	1802	1335		
101	550	713	278	472	1414	400	317	1714	1345		
102	*	2709	279	734	1610	403	310	2400			
108	210	2711	280	581	1611	683	890	1705			
109	209	2711	289	307	103	781					
112	*	2710	292	3078	102	842	3013	1605			
117	341	901	293	727	110	843	3012	1606			
118	340	902	295	726	109	846	936	1507			
122	3807	2702	297	973	105	847	928	1805			
127	823	1008	298	972	107	850	926	1707			
137	798	911	300	677	111	856	370	1509			
139	797	912	303	742	114	858	524	1512			
140	3755	910	305	743	109	871	3041	806			
145	799	910	306	725	2514	876	503	1703			
146	798	911	307	783	2514	877	502	1205			
147	797	912	309	781	2213	878	501	1205			
149	336	1006	311	977	2301	879	500	1204			
150	823	1007	314	741	203	885	739	2014			
152	939	1009	316	740	202	887	3046	2206			
160	813	1105	323	722	307	888	3045	2112			
161	826	1012	326	720	309	889	610	2105			

ABOUT THE AUTHOR

Margaret Major

Margaret Major has practised embroidery for many years and, having a keen interest in dolls' houses, decided to take up miniature embroidery. In 2001 Margaret gained a qualification in miniature embroidery and has subsequently taught the craft from her home in a small, picturesque village in the south-east of England. In addition to her teaching, Margaret exhibits her work at dolls' house and needlecraft fairs. Margaret has written one book previously for GMC Publications: *Miniature Embroidered Patchwork: Projects in 1/12 Scale.*

INDEX

GMC Publications
Castle Place, 166 High Street, Lewes, East Sussex, BN7 1XU, United Kingdom

Tel: 01273 488005 Fax: 01273 402866
E-mail: pubs@thegmcgroup.com
Website: www.gmcbooks.com

Contact us for a complete catalogue, or visit our website.
Orders by credit card are accepted.